A Renaissance
of the Spirit

A Renaissance of the Spirit

A New Way to See Ourselves

Mary Scott

*This publication made possible with
the assistance of the Kern Foundation*

The Theosophical Publishing House
Wheaton, Ill. U.S.A.
Madras, India/London, England

The Theosophical Publishing House
306 West Geneva Road
Wheaton, IL 60187
A publication of the Theosophical Publishing House, a department of the Theosophical Society in America.

Library of Congress Cataloging in Publication Data

Scott, Mary.
A renaissance of the spirit.
  "This publication made possible with the assistance of the Kern Foundation."
  Bibliography: p.
  1. Occultism.   2. Body, Human--Miscellanea.
I. Title.
BF1999.S368   1988   133.8   87-40525
ISBN 0-8356-0632-5 (pbk.)

Printed in the United States of America

To Dr. George Miller, osteopath,
in memory of his great skill and kindness

Contents

Preface

*F*or some time I have been searching for a conceptual framework that could make sense of a number of unusual experiences that science cannot yet explain. This book has developed from that search. Some of these experiences have been my own; some have been those of others who have been at a loss to explain them or have explained them in ways with which I have not always agreed. What I needed was a system of ideas that would encompass them all without violating what I had come to believe as a result of professional training and a great deal of private study.

Perhaps the most teasing phenomenon, met in a variety of contexts, is our apparent possession of more than one body. For many of us this problem never arises. It is very real, however, to those who see specters of people who are dead or are known to be somewhere else or for people who have found themselves looking down on their own bodies in near-death experiences and other unusual states. Psychologists are often told of such experiences. Most of them assume them to be either signs of mental disorder or the hallucinatory byproducts of chemical changes in the brain. This can be true of such diseases as schizophrenia and epilepsy or under anesthesia, but it does not explain genuine cases of what has come to be known as extrasensory perception. These still remain to challenge our scientific understanding.

This was my feeling when, in 1972, I was offered the Oliver Lodge Research Grant by the College of Psychic Studies in London. By that time I had met a great many people, some obviously hallucinated and disturbed, but others trying to make sense of genuine experiences that they were unable to explain. This award set me on the path of serious research and provided me with an opportunity to examine writings on the subject to see if I could come up with a coherent account of multiple bodies that made some sort of scientific sense. The outcome was a small monograph, *Science and Subtle Bodies,* which did not satisfy me but at least helped me to clarify in my own mind some of the issues involved. Between 1975 when the monograph was published and 1981 when I began writing *Kundalini in the Physical World* my problem widened. I now felt challenged not only by the phenomenon of multiple bodies but by parapsychology in general. I could not feel happy with such concepts as "supernature" which seemed only to perpetuate the split between parapsychology and science, a split that surely should not exist at all. The framework I sought was one that would make such concepts unnecessary.

As happens so often in life, I came across the sort of conceptual framework I wanted when looking for something else. In this case I discovered Tantric Hinduism in the course of research into the origins of the concept of kundalini. Kundalini is usually considered to be a force that resides in a center, or *chakra*, at the base of the human spine. With the increasing use in the West of meditation and associated yogic practices, phenomena were being reported that were being called kundalini experiences. Doctors and psychiatrists were beginning to research these experiences, some of which were highly disturbing. It occurred to me to wonder how far we were justified in associating these phenomena with kundalini as this force is described in the Sanskrit source material. It also seemed to me important that medicine should not borrow a word from the East and then misuse it. In *Kundalini in the Physical World* my preoccupation was necessarily with kundalini itself. Nevertheless, while exploring its place in Tantric literature, I got an idea of how forces could interact in a multidimensional universe in a way that would be both scientifically feasible and also explain the phenomenon of multiple bodies.

This only set me on my way, however. It was necessary to see how the model survived when tested against the evidence psychic researchers were trying to explain. In particular, I needed to see how well it explained the various unusual experiences of which I had firsthand knowledge. This book, therefore, as with my earlier work, is in the nature of a progress report on a continuing personal search for an integral philosophy of experience. It is primarily aimed at sharing ideas that may crossfertilize those of others traveling the same road. It does not offer a definitive explanation; it only attempts to arrange material that appears germane in ways that seem to explain the facts of experience better than any I have come across so far.

The book, as it developed, enabled me for the first time to incorporate into an account of a search for explanations some reference to the effects of my pilgrimage upon my own spiritual development and my practice as a psychologist. People who had worked with me had often asked me to write a book about my work. I was never able to do it. The time never seemed right, and the book refused to be written. Perhaps this was because the way I worked and the pilgrimage I was making could not really be separated. And perhaps the same is true of those who worked with me. They were also pilgrims, and what I was giving them was what so many writers, thinkers, and patients had given me: insights and encouragement that kept me going when times were hard and at the same time enlarged my vision and warmed my heart with the knowledge that none of us travels the way alone.

1

The Modern Renaissance

*I*f one can stand aside for a moment from the stress and violence, the greedy affluence and desperate famine, the civil wars and uneasy coexistences and look below the apparent chaos and failure of humanity to cope, one can discover a sense of living through a new Renaissance. In the Middle Ages people stood in humility before the universe, moved instinctively with the seasons, and felt themselves to be in the hands of a Creator who, all the vicissitudes of life notwithstanding, knew what He was doing. What we call the laws of nature they called the will of God; what post–Renaissance society has tried increasingly to dominate and use, pre–Renaissance society tried to understand and adjust to. It is fashionable nowadays to smile at the naiveté with which our ancestors accepted the station in life to which God had called them and to consider ourselves superior to the tribal societies in which people accept roles imposed upon them by the mores of the group, mores that appear to deprive the individual of freedom of choice and that have remained unchanged over hundreds, even thousands, of years.

What did the people of the first Renaissance know that we need a second to rediscover? Why is the world in such difficulties when we are so knowledgeable and technologically advanced? These are questions that we need to face and try to answer if we are not to destroy in one century of technology a globe that our ancestors kept intact for us for millions of years. Why, with all their shortcomings, did they succeed in maintaining the natural order while we, with all our insight into its laws, have destroyed so much in so short a time?

To say that we have grown greedy, comfort-loving, and materialistic is to describe symptoms of a disease, not to diagnose the disease itself. Materialism and greed are rife, of course, but so are religious and esoteric sects. The one can be as divisive as the other. If material greed divides people into we-they categories and generates the rat-race, can there be anything which has been more dehumanizing down the centuries than the we-they dichotomies found in "wars of religion" and clashes of political ideologies intolerantly and fanatically espoused.

If we consider the medieval Renaissance, we find that it is associated with an interesting phrase, "the revival of learning." It was essentially a return to previously existing ways of thinking, the releasing of one of Koestler's "blocked matrices," not an entirely new departure. It was triggered by the rediscovery of classical Greek and Roman philosophy, particularly the former, in which for the first time in the West a great culture began to speculate about man and the universe in logical and not purely mythological terms. The concept in Greek science replaced the symbol. In the symbol reason and imagination, concept and paradox, combine, and many universes of meaning and ways of knowing can blend and overlap. Myths are expanded symbols, statements unfolding a wealth of meanings too complex for a single symbol fully to contain. The Greek achievement, to which Renaissance man fell heir, was to separate reason from emotion, to analyze knowledge and distinguish different modes of knowing. The Greeks were the first Western rationalists, the first humanists, though far from being the first to think creatively about man's place in the cosmos. The thinkers of the medieval Renaissance did for the modern world what the Greeks did for antiquity: they divorced scientific from religious thinking, the concept from the myth. What they did not do was to reject one in favor of the other. It would not have occurred to Leonardo da Vinci any more than to Plato to say "God is dead." The freethinker of the Middle Ages, like his Greek counterpart, knew instinctively the terrible price one pays for hubris, the arrogance that pulls the gods out of the sky and construes "Man, the measure of all things" as "Man, the master of all things." Both were able to stand humbly before nature and keep alive their great religious myths while developing objectivity and scientific modes of thought.

Here we come to the heart of the matter. Somewhere along the line between Leonardo da Vinci and today, hubris has crept in and the creative imagination has lost out. Not only God but the myth is being killed, and we are asked to live on rational ideas and materialistic satisfactions alone. Fortunately, some of our wisest thinkers are recognizing the stultifying effect of this situation not only on the world at large but also on the role of knowledge as a search for truth. In an article in the *British Medical Journal*, "Medicine versus Science," Lord Platt points to pride as the greatest of all blocks to the advancement of learning; science and technology can in a very real sense be enemies of medicine. If the healer becomes infected by scientific hubris and forgets that, while technology is his tool, he is himself the tool of the "wholemaker," he not only begins to focus attention on illness instead of health but loses sight of the whole person in a preoccupation with the body.

During a working life concerned with problems of health and sickness both in individuals and in groups, I have seen stress and frustration mount and "advanced" societies break apart almost in phase with the growth of science and technology. Why is this? It is popular to lay the blame on stress, but stress is as much a necessary part of life as is pain and effort. In fact, it contains an element of both, being at the same time a warning and a response to challenge. The problem lies in determining where and when stress becomes maladaptive. The critical point for any particular individual must come when he or she is confronted for too long by a challenge that cannot be met with the personal resources at hand. How a person breaks down depends on whether the pressures exerted are physical or psychological and where he is constitutionally weakest. If his physiological condition is poor, the body is more likely to give way; if his personality structure is loose or unstable, the psyche is more likely to prove unequal to the struggle. This fact was also true for earlier generations. It is not that we are under greater stress so much as that the causes of stress are different. Nor can we anathematize science and technology, which are neutral in themselves. The problems that they are generating lie in ourselves, with the ways we are using them. Part of the modern renaissance must include a wiser approach to ourselves and our resources both within and without.

We need to recover the Renaissance thinker's ability to pursue knowledge without arrogance, from within the natural order and not in opposition to it. We need a concept of objectivity that does not divide mind from matter, observer from observed, in a way that splits reality into two parts different in kind. We need a world view that not only unifies mind and matter but one that takes the human spirit into account. So many modern stresses have their roots in a spiritual hunger for wholeness, not only in the world but in ourselves.

These are the challenges that we have to meet if we are to see the fulfillment of a modern renaissance and not the death of a planet. If man is indeed the measure of all things, the climax of an evolutionary process, we may learn more about nature, the great galactic fields, and even whether there is purpose or randomness at the heart of creation, by studying our own potentialities than by trying to force ourselves into ideological straitjackets that obviously do not fit while striving after technological advances at a pace too fast for many of us. The man in the street is protesting against his leadership and his artificial way of life by every means stress and frustration can devise. This is obvious if we would only look at him with seeing eyes. The Greeks had a word for what we need: *metanoia,* a word that wonderfully combines the notions of contrition for past misjudgments and the ability to see with fresh vision the error of our ways.

It is not enough to worry about crime in terms of suppressing it or to try to allay anxieties about nuclear deterrents and industrial pollution by economic and political arguments. To do this is to treat symptoms without probing for causes, for the reasons why people are protesting in so many ways about so many aspects of life. Short-term, piecemeal policies aimed at papering over the cracks developing in society are no substitute for the metanoia that is what we really need. That way we only run the risk of total breakdown. What is necessary is to see ourselves and our entire situation in a completely new way.

There is growing evidence that we are beginning to move in this direction. Narrow conceptions of human nature and materialistic presuppositions about the universe are gradually being discarded under pressures from within science itself, notably in the fields of fundamental physics, psychobiology, and holistic medicine. Grass-roots protest groups are becoming better informed and more insistent in their demands for changes in the way society is organized and the values on which it is based. It is not generally recognized how many people are unemployed not because they are lazy or unskilled but because they are not prepared to acquire skills that only serve to prop up a social organization with which they can no longer identify. Many young people are rootless for want of leaders able to appeal to their idealism and harness its vitality. They need to be given goals that can release their creativity by giving them new and more inspiring perspectives on the future.

Above all, they want to be able to see the world and their place in it in ways that unify people and not divide them and that satisfy their spiritual hunger for wholeness without laying them open to hubris. Under the influence of the first Renaissance, Galileo and Copernicus ousted the earth from the center of the universe and replaced it with the sun. We, I think, must face the task of placing mankind there—but mankind as Plato and Leonardo saw it, as a hologram of the universe, the measure of all things.

To achieve this new vision, we must be prepared to probe our own natures with profound humility, using the combined tools of reason and imagination, concept and symbol, science and art. Already we are borrowing widely from the older cultures of the East and the Americas, as once we borrowed from classical Greece and Rome, creating a pool of ideas and images on which to draw. All these lie like tesserae, ready to hand alongside the data of science. It is the mosaic that one feels is being put together, sometimes consciously, sometimes unconsciously, by creative people all over the world that gives one the sense of renaissance. This rebirth of the human spirit has an exciting new dimension: it must be global. We must all be involved, not just the peoples of the Western world. If at present our situation looks chaotic, so does an artist's palette as a picture takes form.

2

Widening Science

*T*he metanoia discussed in the previous chapter involves no less than a reassessment of our ideas, both scientific and political, about what is implied by being human. It also involves a reevaluation of science as an appropriate tool for studying man as a thinking species able to function on a wide range of behavioral levels and to be conscious in a wide variety of ways. The materialistic assumptions of orthodox science leave far too many experiences unexplained and unusual abilities discounted as either fraudulent or evidence of morbidly dissociated states. Nevertheless there is a growing demand for them to be explained. An increasing number of intelligent and qualified people are interesting themselves in extrasensory perception and the psychobiology of such phenomena as mediumship and telekinesis. There are also psychologists, biologists, and physicists whose work is progressively forcing them out of the laboratory into abstract speculation about possible entities needed to explain the relation between mind and matter in human beings and in the universe at large.

9

Philosophers of science are also coming to realize that science does not deal directly with the outside world, with hard facts; rather, it deals with perceptions, with the outside world as it is represented in sensory experience. This remains true whatever methodologies scientists employ and however broadly or narrowly they define their roles. In the last analysis it is not the universe but our experience of it that needs to be explained. It is because the universe is ultimately a human experience that man is the measure of all things.

If only for this reason we need a more complete and satisfying working model of ourselves and the universe that we experience. Our minds need to move more freely in a wider world than the purely physical one that the materialists offer us. We need scientists and philosophers who will help us to do this, men and women who are broad-minded in the best sense, people who are prepared to venture into unconventional areas and study unusual happenings in their search for truth. Indeed, all of us need to break out of the straitjackets that materialism has imposed upon us. Perhaps the worst casualties of this century's technological revolution have been aesthetic and spiritual insight. So much that enriched the lives of past generations has become "mere superstition" or "just imagination." We no longer recognize genuine experiences native to us as human beings that were taken for granted in earlier times. These losses are grievous; and if we do not make them good, illness, apathy, and despair can only generate even more violence in our troubled world. It is simply not true that mankind and the universe are as circumscribed as we have been indoctrinated to believe. The social stresses that are pulling us apart are largely due to frustrations of spirit. If we are to break out of our straitjackets, we need some more holistic conception of what science is all about. The Age of Reason played an important part in shaping the modern world but at the expense of much that the thinkers of the first Renaissance sought to give us.

A useful concept from which to start developing a truly integral theory of the human universe as it is actually experienced is that of fields. Fundamental physics has already familiarized us with the notion of the physical universe as a system of interlocking fields patterned by the electromagnetic and gravitational forces that hold it together. We need to expand this idea to include levels of energy supplementing those of the electromagnetic spectrum. One cannot think seriously of a human being as merely a body surrounded by an electromagnetic field. In order to account for thinking, emotion, and other human functions, one must assume there are other finer energies interacting with those of our physical body. The forces of life and mind must work in us in much more complex energy patterns to account for the range of experiences and behaviors of which we are capable.

Part of sloughing off our straitjackets could lie in thinking of ourselves and our world as comprising many energy levels, each with its own waveband, extending from the forces of densest matter to those of finest spirit. It is surely not so difficult to envisage thought as a force or the spirit as having power. It only requires that we accustom ourselves to thinking of everything in terms of energy and communication—which is where science itself has led us. It has reduced all matter to energy, and its conception of a unified field suggests that all parts of the universe are ultimately in communication with one another. All we have to do is to widen science, to enlarge our field of fields, our spectrum of energies.

The findings of H. S. Burr and L. L. Vasiliev have been urging us in this direction since the 1920s and 1930s without receiving sufficient response from the scientific establishment. Burr was Hunt Professor of Anatomy at Yale Medical School. Using a voltmeter of his own invention, he showed that there are energy fields around living things that actually control them. He called them "fields of life." Working with his colleague, Dr. F. S. C. Northrop, in the 1930s he discovered that all living entities, whether organisms or their component parts, are accompanied by measurable fields,variations of which modify their shape and manner of growth. It is these which maintain them in specific forms in spite of constant changes in the dense matter of which they are composed. Life, in other words, works through fields. They published their results in an article entitled, *The Electrodynamic Theory of Life"* in 1935. It did not arouse the interest it deserved. Scientists at that time were unwilling to accept some of the implications of Burr's experiments, and his work is still less influential than it ought to be. It has applications that could be usefully employed not only in medicine, but in agriculture, family planning, and other socially important areas.

The experimental work that he and his colleagues carried out over thirty years is summarized by Burr in *Blueprint for Immortality*. It is also discussed by the scientific journalist Edward Russell in *Design for Destiny* in an attempt to make it more generally known. The body of work covers many subjects, including the electrodynamic patterns of men and women in various states of health and disease and the way in which degrees of hypnotic trance produce a voltage gradient in the life field. It reports on seasonal fluctuations in the field patterns of trees and shows how the fields of seeds and eggs already carry information about their inherent potential. An interesting discovery that could be put to good use by the infertile was the fact that, just before ovulation, there is a general rise in the field voltage of women. That the change in the field preceded the change in the body led Burr and his colleagues to realize that field measurements had a predictive value for the diagnosis and treatment of suspected disorders in plants and animals as well as in humans.

From the standpoint of traditional science the troublesome implications of Burr's findings arise from the fact that fields are exceedingly stable and preserve their identity over long distances and periods of time, but they must have a source to induce them. Materialists would like that source to lie in the chemical body, but the predictive element in Burr's measurements indicates that field changes precede bodily changes and appear to determine them. They imply that even the simplest organism is more than field and form. There is a source of both that is neither physically nor chemically material, at least in the sense that "material" is commonly understood. This is the finding that or-

thodox science is unable to explain and that cannot be explained without some more comprehensive field theory. Vasiliev's findings make this even
clearer.

Vasiliev was Professor of Physiology at the University of Leningrad. With an impressive team of
colleagues he carried out a classical series of experiments on telepathy, which extended from 1921 to
just before World War II. The English physicist, W.
F. Barrett had first attempted to tackle the problem
at a conference of the British Association for the Advancement of Science in 1876. Subsequently the
Society for Psychical Research was set up in London in 1882 to collect and study ostensibly authen-
tic cases. The results were published by Gurney,
Myers, and Podmore in *Phantasms of the Living* in
1886; it was here that the term "telepathy" was first
used. The authors divided the study into an examination of spontaneous and experimentally induced
phenomena. It is in the second category that the
Russian experiments belong, though they were
done less to verify the phenomenon than to verify
the theory that thought transmission involved some
form of electromagnetic radiation emanating from
one brain and received by another.

The details of the methods used and the conclu-
sions reached were written up by Vasiliev in *Experiments in Mental Suggestion*, translated into
English by Anita Kohsen and C. C. L. Gregory in
1963 with the author's blessing. It is a very technical
and rigorously academic monograph with a great
deal of learned commentary, which makes it difficult to summarize. The openness to criticism, the

readiness to use it to refine experimental techniques, and the inherent modesty of the true scientist so inform it, however, that it is well worth tackling its difficulties.

The research team with which Vasiliev worked in Leningrad was very high-powered. It was composed of physiologists, physicists, a philosopher, a medical hypnotist, an engineer, and a host of specialist consultants including experts in radio technology. Their initial aim was to analyze the wavelengths of the electromagnetic radiations involved in thought-transmission processes. First, they had to confirm that electromagnetism was indeed involved. To this end Vasiliev and his colleagues set out to construct a metal chamber along the lines of a Faraday cage, through which such radiation could not pass. By placing either the sender or the recipient in this chamber while the other was outside, it was soon found that the telepathic process was in no way impeded. Whatever energy was involved, it was not electromagnetism. Whether or not the transfer of thought took place appeared to depend on psychological factors, notably on the power of the sender to concentrate and visualize and on the recipient's sensitivity to suggestion. The experiments were also found to be more successful and easier to control if subjects were in a hypnotized state. Another surprising finding was that the one essential condition of success was that the recipient be known to the sender. They had anticipated that the direction in which thought was "beamed" would be important. This did not prove to be the case, nor did it seem necessary for the sender to know where the recipient was. This was demonstrated by a repeatable experiment in which the sender had no idea where the experiment was being carried out. It was shown that, provided that the sender could both envisage the recipient and concentrate on the material to be transmitted at the same time, the experimental environment was quite immaterial.

An interesting experiment that showed how clearly defined a thought field can be was one in which a sender instructed two different subjects to go to sleep. One subject was in the mental chamber with the sender, and the other in another room in the laboratory. So long as the sender concentrated on the recipient outside sufficiently strongly the one beside him would continue sleeping, whereas the other woke up. This shows that the fields generated by thought can clearly overlap without interfering with one another, as each seems to be specifically controlled by the focus of attention. That fields are involved is shown by the linking of two spatially unconnected things, in this case two human beings, or as Vasiliev and his colleagues would say, two suitably tuned brains.

That distance made no difference to the transmission process provided that sender and recipient were competent performers was shown in another series of experiments. These were ingeniously contrived to eliminate all clues from other sources, including preknowledge on the part of the experimenter-observer of when the transmission was to take place. The distance varied from the next room to as far away as Sebastopol, roughly 1,000 miles from Leningrad. Moreover, it was found that time was not a variable. Under hypnotic conditions it took recipients between one and two and one-half minutes to respond to the instruction to wake up, whether they were in Sebastopol or Leningrad. When subjects were not hypnotized, reaction times were much longer and depended on differential rates of response among recipients.

Vasiliev recognized that the team was not dealing with electromagnetic energy but realized that some field force was at work. As he wrote in the concluding chapter of his monograph:

> Of course everything which exists in the universe is not yet understood. Now micro-fields are being discovered not exceeding the boundaries of the atom: could one not suppose that sooner or later a new macro-field will be discovered which will go beyond the boundaries of atoms and engulf the surrounding space?

Some outstanding foreign scientists are already focusing their research in this direction. For instance, Pascal Jordan, the German physicist and Nobel Prize–winner, and Dr. B. Hoffman, a former collaborator of Einstein, think that the gravitational field seems to have some similarity with the force that transmits telepathic information in that both act at a distance and penetrate all obstacles. Edward Russell, the American scientific journalist who did so much to popularize the field experiments and findings of Burr and Vasiliev, christened Burr's fields of life L-fields and Vasiliev's fields of thought T-fields. As he points out in *Design for Destiny*, fields take many forms and sizes in nature and also in man-made contrivances. Even if T-fields originate in some minute cerebral area, as Vasiliev thought, they can extend over as yet unlimited distances. They may also be able to attach themselves to objects, as the ancient practices of blessing and magnetizing amulets have long implied. The art of psychometry, which enables the sensitive to gather information about their owners by handling objects, similarly assumes something in the nature of T-fields to be selectively registered by his probing mind. However, as noted by Vasiliev, a specific mental set is needed before the psychometrist can start work. Provided that the set is right and attention is concentrated on a particular person, the psychometrist's search can be successful. Someone's watch, for instance, may have passed through many hands. It is the attention of the person who wants the information and of the sensitive that ensures that only the relevant T-field is selected out of the full range of T-fields that have been attached to the watch at different times by different people.

Readers of S. Ostrander and L. Schroeder's book *Psychic Discoveries Behind the Iron Curtain* will know how much money and effort the Eastern-bloc countries have put into the development not only of telepathy but of other psychic gifts in order that they may be put to practical use. Likely subjects are encouraged to improve their skills as clairvoyants, dowsers, precognitive experts, and mind-over-matter sensitives able to move objects about without touching them. There are training schools for sensitives in several Eastern bloc countries—in an avowedly materialist society and with the blessing of the authorities. This official attitude goes back to Stalin, who once had a star telepathist whisked off the stage of a theater in Byelorussia in order to answer questions about what was going on in Poland. Stalin also assigned the same man the task of entering his country house unharmed and without a pass. He did this to Stalin's satisfaction by the simple expedient of mentally suggesting to the numerous guards that he was Beria, at that time head of the KGB.

K. E. Tsiolkovski, the father of Russian rocketry, said in the 1930s that in the coming era of space flight telepathic abilities would be necessary. He held that rockets would bring knowledge of the secrets of the universe but that the study of psychic phenomena would give us knowledge of the mysteries of the human mind. Some Soviet scientists even think of telepathy as the common language of all cosmonauts, both human and possible visitors from outer space. They claim that they would like to equip their astronauts with ESP techniques as well as with the electronic gadgetry. In this the Soviets are far ahead of us in the West and are arguably spending their money more wisely. They are, however, no further ahead in following up the implications of their own researches.

An important aspect of the concept of fields is that it can carry our thinking outwards in two directions, toward the source that induces the field and toward the dense matter that it organizes. Taken as a whole, we have a tripartite phenomenon to explore, one that takes us into the psychological realm in search of sources and into chemistry to discover what it organizes and how it organizes it. Fields do not belong only to physics. They belong in science as an integral study involving psychology as inevitably as they involve chemistry and physics. Psychology may not be necessary to explain some chemical and physical fields, but if there is a mental component influencing such fields, it is vital not to exclude it. It is here that the materialist errs in attempting to reduce mind to brain, psychology to physiology. If the bioenergetic field precedes the chemical changes it induces, the body cannot be its source. If the psychoenergetic field induces changes in the brain via the life fields, it also must have a source. Field theory, by carrying our thought onward in this way, brings us to the conclusion that, as far as human beings are concerned, the source of all fields must lie in the living, thinking individual whose fields they are.

For a pragmatic body the Soviet academic establishment wastes an unconscionable amount of time trying to find a narrowly materialistic explanation of ESP and other psychic gifts. The ideological commitment of the Eastern bloc to materialism and to a relatively inflexible political theory is a great tragedy for science and the world. We can surely have a unitary, multidimensional world without insisting on its being a chemicophysical one.

Materialism as generally understood is based on the assumption that everything is either physical or the result of movements in something physical. It is a theory that evolved as a result of the principle of parsimony. Science in its early stages was well advised to avoid the unnecessary multiplication of entities and concentrate on what could be observed and measured. It is always wise to keep one's speculations rooted in verifiable experience. What is not so wise is arbitrarily to define what that experience must be in advance of or in spite of the data. Both atheism and materialism are in fact assumptions resting as much on faith rather than proof as are theism or religious fundamentalism. It is as unscientific, for instance, to say there is no God because one has not experienced such a being as to say there is no such thing as a rhinoceros because one has never seen one. In science nothing is impossible in principle; a closed mind is an essentially unscientific one. Our limitations are in ourselves, and our misfortune is that we too often impose them upon experience, thus unconsciously restricting the range of our insight.

As with undisciplined speculation, so also with the loose use of words. For all its pedantic excesses, semantic philosophy has been as salutary as materialism. We would be wise in furthering our renaissance to give careful consideration to problems of terminology. Terms used differently by different groups engender misunderstanding and unnecessary duplication of effort and impede the development of common frames of reference. We need to strive after a shared vocabulary in each new area of knowledge as it opens up. Our moves in this direction, however, should not be forced. Differences of usage among different groups can be useful and stimulating when science is venturing into unfamiliar territory because each research worker approaches phenomena from a slightly different angle and may pick up something others have overlooked. Humility before nature and before the contributions of others well becomes the scholar in any discipline.

It is easy to assume that the other chap is simply wrong but more fruitful to question why you think so.

When reading *Psychic Discoveries behind the Iron Curtain,* one is struck by the variety of terms chosen by scientists in the Soviet Union and in Czechoslovakia to connote various paranormal phenomena. There are similar variations of usage in the West. I think that the Eastern bloc's preference for "psychotronics" over "parapsychology" has a lot to be said for it. It suggests interdisciplinary cooperation, combining as it does the concepts of psychology, physics, and energy. I have never been very happy with the "para" approach, the verbal casting out from mother disciplines of phenomena waiting to be understood. In spite of the fact that "ESP" has become common usage, along with an increasing number of others I am dubious about the term. It seems far more likely that we all have sensibilities that are either latent or dormant than that some have special senses that others lack, the mechanisms of which lie outside the nervous system or sensory perception as a whole.

Interdisciplinary projects hold many terminological traps for the unwary. This is due to the development of specialized branches of knowledge in comparative isolation from one another. Some have borrowed words from ordinary speech and given them new meanings; others have borrowed the same words from Greek or Latin and applied them differently. Words are also entering the language from oriental sources; still others are drawn from the occult writings of the various theosophical schools without always being used in the same way. If scholars, particularly scientists, insist upon interpreting the work of others in terms of their own specialist languages, we shall never be able to create a single universe of discourse within which we can discuss man and the cosmos with some degree of common understanding. For the foreseeable future we will have to pick our way through terminological complexities, which means that we must be prepared to treat our linguistic differences as foreign languages that need to be translated and interpreted and make allowances for our mutual misuse of one another's languages in the meantime.

3

Extended Sense Perception

*D*r. Shafica Karagulla uses the term "higher sense perception" rather than "extrasensory perception." Dr. Karagulla has been studying psychic phenomena for more than thirty years. She was born in Turkey and educated in Beirut, where she qualified as a doctor of medicine at the American University Medical School. She went on to train as a psychiatrist at the Royal Hospital for Mental and Nervous Disorders at Edinburgh in Scotland before going to Canada on a research fellowship in the department of neurology and neurosurgery at McGill University. For three and one-half years she worked as psychiatric consultant in association with Dr. Wilder Penfield, the famous neurosurgeon and geographer of the brain. In 1957 she became an associate professor in the department of psychiatry at the State University of New York. She was just about to accept another university appointment when she was asked if she would read a "rather unusual book with an open mind." It was Joseph Millard's *Edgar Cayce, Mystery Man of Miracles.* Edgar Cayce was a healer who used to diagnose and treat patients while in a self-induced state of semitrance. As a specialist with wide experience of hallucinations and illusions, she was asked if she could explain Cayce's gifts in medical terms.

At the outset she expected to find some underlying cerebral abnormality. To her surprise, she found nothing that she could trace to any form of morbidity. It became increasingly clear to her that she was dealing with someone with very unusual abilities. The Cayce material is extensive and well documented, but by this time Cayce was dead and could not be interviewed. Fortunately, the friend who had introduced her to Millard's book was herself a sensitive and could put Karagulla in touch with a number of other gifted people who were willing to talk confidentially to a qualified physician.

Those familiar with the literature of parapsychology and psychical research will be interested in the number of highly intelligent and prominent people who rely on clairvoyance, clairaudience, clairsentience, telepathy, psychometry, telekinesis, magnetic healing, far-memory of past lives, and precognition to enhance their ordinary working skills. The great majority do not mention the fact for fear of appearing odd, though many do not realize how unusual their abilities are because they take them so much for granted.

In her book *Breakthrough to Creativity* Dr. Karagulla presents us with a rich array of case histories. They are arresting not only because they reveal how prevalent these gifts are in our society but because of the insight they give us into special acuities of perception. Karagulla's subjects use their gifts because they work, because their "psychic" perceptions are continually verified in their daily lives. It is important to distinguish between this type of perceptual experience and the subjective experiences of depth psychology. The "inner" world of Karagulla's subjects is only an inner world in the sense that most people cannot perceive it. There is what she calls a "five-senses barrier" that prevents most of us from entering it. For those who can, however, it seems to be objective in the same way that the ordinary world is objective except that one is freer in it, both in terms of time and space, than one is when using the five senses.

Karagulla found people with higher sense perception (HSP) in sufficient numbers to wonder whether they represented a mutation in the nature of consciousness. Of this I am doubtful. Data from history and anthropology suggest that the type of "supersensitivity" she found in her subjects has existed from very early times among the elite of both simple and sophisticated societies. As Puharich has shown in *Beyond Telepathy* and Castaneda in his *Don Juan* books, shamans and medicine men and women have used various techniques to heighten their capacity for HSP, but there is also evidence that they can exercise their gifts in normal states of consciousness. The Australian aborigines' social use of telepathy and clairvoyance clearly goes back into prehistory, so much is it part of their way of life, and they belong to one of the oldest races on earth. The priests and priestesses of antiquity were not all of the mediumistic, Delphic variety, and the entire prophetic tradition rests upon the seer's ability to enter a higher perceptual realm. What Dr.

Karagulla is recognizing, I think, is not so much a mutation in the biological sense as a renaissance in Western society, a resurgence into our scientific world of knowledge and skills lost in the Dark Ages because they were associated with paganism in the minds of the early Church Fathers.

Perhaps not surprisingly, those who came to see Karagulla were often doctors themselves. Many were glad, even relieved, to talk about their experiences to an unprejudiced member of their own profession. Of these Karagulla writes:

> The different physicians with whom I talked showed a wide spectrum of HSP ability. I felt that many of them probably had more than they realized. For the most part they stumbled on the recognition of their unusual abilities with little understanding of their possibilities. Some used them effectively and with confidence because of years of experience. Usually they made no special effort to increase their potential or discover other possibilities of its use.

This could partly be, as she writes further, because

> . . . they feared any mention of such things might hurt their professional standing. In most cases each felt that he was perhaps alone and peculiar.

Some of the forms of HSP found among physicians involved seeing, others sensing, and still others the direct kind of knowing found in intuition and some types of telepathy. Quite a number spoke of force fields, energies that they could see around and interpenetrating the body. Some saw these as a complex of forces moving along the nerves and running into blockages in states of ill-health. Others could also see the actual organs threatened by disease. Still others saw a wider aura and vortices of energy along the spine apparently corresponding to the *chakras* described in treatises on Tantric yoga. While some saw what was wrong with their patients, others sensed areas of morbidity either by feeling sympathetic pain in corresponding parts of their own bodies or by touch through their hands. One unfortunate physician was so telepathically en rapport with his patients that he was virtually on duty twenty-four hours a day. A few could judge from a person's force field not only what was wrong but what the prognosis was likely to be. These prognoses were based on the fact that specific changes in the body had been found to follow changes in the force field and so could be anticipated. This suggests that the voltmeter invented by H. S. Burr, which he claimed could be predictive, was measuring what these doctors could sense.

Not all HSP takes place in ordinary space. Like Cayce, some doctors found that they could diagnose patients at a distance by means of far-viewing, using the eyes of the mind. Other subjects reported diagnosis involving precognition, which implies a degree of freedom in time as well. The difference between precognition and planning and anticipating is that it is a way of knowing about the future in advance, not a manipulation of images as if the future were now. It brings with it varying degrees of certainty. Some precognitive experiences are the most tenuous of hunches; others are clear pictorial or symbolic statements or intuitions with the ring of truth about them. What validates them is that the events foreseen actually occur. How a sensitive presumes them to be precognitive seems largely a matter of practice and experience. The observation of recurring correlations seems to have been how most of Dr. Karagulla's subjects came to rely on their HSP abilities and use them.

These HSP capacities would seem to be no more "paranormal" than certain animal skills that we find difficult to understand, such as the navigational prowess of migrating birds and spawning salmon. They are, however, less obviously genetically based and appear to be much more influenced by social factors. From oriental writings it is clear that the various forms of HSP mentioned by Karagulla have long been known. The task of gurus included teaching their pupils how to develop and use them. As the *Don Juan* books show, the same is true of shamans. Unlike Karagulla's subjects, however, nothing in their cultures prevents yogis and shamans from taking such gifts for granted and making constructive use of them.

Another category of experiences that any holistic account of human nature has to explain is our apparent possession of more "bodies" than the familiar physical one. Those who have had such experiences are often disbelieved. This is because the phenomenon is largely subjective, which makes it easy for doctors and scientists to write it off as "just imagination." It is very real, however, for those who see, as if present, someone who is dead or known to be elsewhere, or for people who find themselves floating near the ceiling of operating theaters looking down on some anesthetized version of themselves or who have out-of-body experiences in other unconscious and semiconscious states. The first experience can be frightening, since it combines the fear of the supernatural with the fear of going mad. Psychologists are often told of such fears. If the phantom is of someone loved who has recently died, once one has calmed down and decided one is relatively sane, it is fairly easy to conclude that grief and imagination have produced a hallucination and let it go at that. But if the apparition appears distressed and to be trying to convey something to us, or if it is a stranger behaving as if one were not there, then it is more difficult to explain the incident away.

I had an experience of the first kind the night after my father died. I was sleeping in his old study as his nurse was still using my room. In the drowsy state that precedes sleep I heard him coming along the passage from my mother's room. Sleepily, I thought that he was locking up as he used to do last thing at night. Instead, he opened the study door and said, "Mollie, tell your mother I am quite all right. Quite all right." With that I woke completely to the knowledge of his death, and he promptly vanished. He must have been coming from my mother's room to mine. Possibly her grief had prevented him from getting through to her, and in my semiconscious state I was the more receptive.

An incident of the second kind happened to a friend of mine. She had been staying in a very old house in Devon, England, when she woke in the night to see a man in period dress walk across the room and out the door. Living in an old and haunted house herself, she was quite blasé about ghosts. This one startled her, however, because he had no feet. "Oh," said her hosts when she reported this event in the morning, "that is because the floor has been raised since his time." For nonchalance she had met her match.

Another group of phenomena that suggests multiple bodies is that of the "auras" seen around people and of the entity often referred to as the "astral body" or "etheric double." Many sensitives, like Karagulla's clairvoyant subjects, claim to see these. I first came across one who put this gift to practical use when I was a teenager. Phoebe Payne was a theosophical friend of my parents. She later married another theosophist, Dr. Laurence Bendit, and used her clairvoyance diagnostically in collaboration with her husband and a group of his medical colleagues. I remember being particularly impressed by her matter-of-fact approach to her gifts. She had apparently been clairvoyant from birth and described how she had to learn to distinguish between what she saw that everyone else saw and what she saw that others did not. She said that she would probably have grown up thoroughly neurotic had her father not come to believe that she had a real gift and not merely an overactive imagination. He helped her to live in two worlds and learn how to switch consciously from one kind of seeing to the other. Her gifts were no doubt much refined by further training in adult life. Her autobiography *Man's Latent Powers* makes clear how valuable her detachment and critical mind were in enabling her to do this. The book *The Psychic Sense* which she wrote in collaboration with her husband in 1943, is well worth reading as an account of a sensitive's struggle to understand her own gift with the help of a medically qualified partner. In *Man Incarnate*, also written in collaboration with her husband, she gives an account of what they called "the vital etheric field," which is responsible for the auras seen surrounding and interpenetrating the physical body. She maintained that there were etheric counterparts of every organ and cell in the body.

Dr. Karagulla had a sensitive, Diane, who could also see auras. Like Mrs. Bendit, she was in complete control of her gifts. Though she was the president of a corporation with a family to care for, she undertook to work with Dr. Karagulla using her ability to see the internal organs of the body and their activities in a program of medical research. She had not studied medicine, but it was not difficult to translate her lay language into medical terms. She could also see a "vital or energy body or field" as a constantly moving "web of light beams" interpenetrating the dense body and extending an inch or two beyond it. She insisted that disturbances in the physical structure were preceded and then accompanied by disturbances in its energy replica. In this she confirms Burr's contention that changes in the life field antedate rather than follow changes in the organs themselves. Karagulla gives a very full account of the energy body as seen by Diane, which interested readers may well want to study for themselves. The most striking outcome of this research program was the close correlation between clairvoyant diagnoses made by Diane and those made by hospital consultants using conventional equipment. There were also predictions made by Diane that could not be medically foreseen and that were later validated by events.

The idea that normally imperceptible energy fields are associated with all living things has been growing steadily for some years within academic circles. Instrumental investigations of the auras surrounding plants and human hands by the use of various photographic techniques have been followed by attempts to plot the body field. Particular interest has centered on the *chakras,* or force centers, that many clairvoyants claim to see in an effort to confirm their existence. So far, they have produced nothing of great diagnostic value. Forces seem to be involved that instruments cannot yet detect.

Another problem that will have to be confronted is the relation between the center of consciousness and the physical body in near-death and out-of-body experiences. Jung gives an account of the experience of one of his patients who nearly died during a particularly difficult birth that shows how objective "second body" experiences can be. In *The Structure and Dynamics of the Psyche* he tells us that the woman, who was in a state of near fatal collapse, was aware not only of her inert physical body but also of the behavior of the medical staff and her anxious relatives. She was particularly struck by the panic exhibited by the doctor, who paced up and down excitedly, apparently having completely lost his head. When she recovered consciousness, the nurse at first energetically denied that the doctor had been hysterical. Only when the patient described in detail what she had seen did the nurse admit that her account agreed exactly with what had taken place. Cases of this sort have been reported over and over again, as the growing literature on near-death experiences amply testifies.

The different ways in which the second body can be perceived by subjects themselves is another area that needs exploring. For some it seemed to be more or less similar to the physical body in shape, suggesting that consciousness may have moved into its energy replica, as is described by Diane and Mrs. Bendit. For some it was as if they were in a sphere or capsule, or as if they were more aware of the boundaries of the aura than of the form of the second body itself. For instance, in Dr. Raymond Moody's collection of case histories of patients resuscitated when near death, *Life after Life*, one patient reported:

> I wasn't in a body as such. I could feel something, some kind of a—like a capsule or something, like a clear form. I couldn't really see it; it was like it was transparent, but not really. It was like I was just there. . . . sort of just like a ball of energy.

Another said:

> I felt I was a round ball and almost maybe like I might have been a little sphere. . . on the inside of this round ball.

In both these cases the center of consciousness seemed to be detached from any body sense. Others, however, were more body-conscious. One said:

> . . . it was like I did come out of my body and go into something else. . . It was another body. . . but not a regular human body. It's a little bit different. . . It had form to it, but no colour. . . Things seem to go faster after you go out of your body.

Another said of this body:

> . . . it felt as if it had a *density* to it, almost, but not a physical density—kind of like waves or some-

thing...Nothing really physical, almost as if it were charged...

This impression of the second body as an energy system rather than a material structure was confirmed by another subject, who said:

> ...I kept getting in and out of my physical body. But, while I did I was still in a body—not a physical body, but something I can best describe as an energy pattern. If I had to put it into words, I would say that it was transparent, a spiritual as opposed to a material being. Yet it definitely had different parts.

From many accounts of out-of-body experiences (OBE) it is clear that time not only goes faster, but there are superphysical degrees of freedom in space. As with near-death experiences (NDE), there seems to be a mobile center of consciousness that moves into another body. Like telepathy, it would seem to operate at another energy level, since it appears to travel less at the speed of light than with the immediacy of thought. Vasiliev contended that thought fields are material, but if they are they are material only if one first equates matter and energy and then thinks of energy in terms of a wider range of frequencies and resonances than is yet customary in science.

From data such as this—and much more that can be found in the considerable literature that now exists on NDE, OBE, shamanism, and astral projection—as it becomes increasingly clear that the mobile center of consciousness is related to but not dependent on the physical brain. It seems rather to be an adjunct of the self that is capable of changing levels according to where the attention of the observing self is currently focused. Readers of Robert Monroe's account of his many self-induced OBEs in *Journeys out of the Body* will know about his experience of a yet finer body into which it moved from time to time. When he was in it he found himself in a realm where the laws of physics no longer applied and thought and intention governed everything, both what he did and how he did it. He describes three levels of consciousness in which he was aware of an embodied self behaving in a variety of ways while his dense "chemical" body lay unconscious on the couch. Obviously, he was only out of his body in a limited sense. Nevertheless, the body he felt himself to be in did not seem to vary. It was the laws governing its behavior that seemed to change so that he described his experiences in terms of different locales rather than different bodies.

From this brief review it can be seen that there is a large quantity of case material ready to hand for holistically minded researchers to draw on— enough, certainly, to help them to frame a more comprehensive account of human beings and the various environments in which they can move.

4

A Higher Center of Control

We in the West not only tend to underestimate our sensory possibilities but also our potential skills. Ostrander and Schroeder give a fascinating account of the work of Vladimir Raikov, who has evolved a technique that he calls "artificial reincarnation." By taking subjects through and beyond the usual state of deep trance he claims that he can hypnotize them into a state of superwakefulness. When this point is reached, he induces them to act out a role, often that of a historic personage. For instance, he "reincarnated" a nineteenth-century Russian painter, Ilya Repin, in a senior science student who was poor at drawing and little interested in art. After twenty-five sessions she was herself able to paint like a professional but, interestingly enough, in a style of her own. On another occasion Raikov used his technique in a different way. He was treating an alcoholic, and, instead of incarnating some well-known person, he successively incarnated into his patient various members of his family in order that self-healing might be induced by experiencing himself as others saw him. This experiment was apparently as successful as the one aimed at releasing creativity.

The social value of such education and reeducation is obvious. Equally obvious are the dangers in its abuse, for, as Ostrander and Schroeder were informed, the potentialities released and the cures effected are stable over time, while the subject has no memory of what happens between going into trance and waking up as his usual self.

There is another aspect of Raikov's work that I find intriguing. Raikov states that before a subject can reincarnate another personality he must go through all the passive, suggestible stages of trance. He then wakes in a new way, as it were, and it is at this point that role-taking begins. Raikov claims that the state induced is one of enhanced consciousness and, once a reincarnation has started, nonsuggestibility. It would be interesting to see Dr. Raikov at work and find out just how he controls the reincarnation process if, once started, something in the subject takes over from him. Ostrander and Schroeder tell the amusing story of his incarnating in a person, presumably one deficient in self-confidence, the forceful character of an English queen. He was treated as the subject of his subject until the session ended, but we are not told how the queen's subject deincarnated the queen and safely returned the pair of them to normality and present time.

I am interested in superwakefulness reached via the deepest trance because it carries with it the suggestion of a center of awareness and control above and beyond that of ordinary ego consciousness. In

1957 Dr. W. V. Cruden of Hove, England, wrote an article entitled *A Study of Wake,* which has not had the influence it deserves. He argued that waking consciousness is not a primary state but rather the cessation of the sleeping state brought about by stimulation and arousal. He points out how readily we drowse when bored and when the body is relaxed, satiated, or fatigued. Being fully conscious and self-directing is not something that we can assume to occur in animals. In *The Living Brain* the late Grey Walter claimed that there is no evidence to suppose that any other creature, not even the chimpanzee, can hold an image in consciousness long enough to manipulate it and so plan ahead. This means that the human ability to remember and imagine is a phylogenetically recent development and therefore biologically more unstable than our sensory abilities and motor skills.

Myself as a self-image, as distinct from the concept of being a separate entity, is an evolutionary product of an even later date. It can complicate as well as facilitate interpersonal relations and social adaptation. When teaching psychology to Ghanian students, I was struck by the tenuous nature of their self-portraits. Compared with British students, they lacked content. The tribal "I" tends to move like an actor from one role to another within a way of life. All of us were probably at one time similarly un-self-conscious, assuming our identities from our roles within the groups to which we belonged. Perhaps once we have learned to handle ourselves better we shall regain this lost art. At present we are so involved in developing individuality, being ourselves, doing our own thing, that we tend to want only roles that suit our ideas of ourselves. As we shall see later, the real "I," the existential ego, as it is sometimes called, is quite distinct from the self that we think we are. The only "I" that is truly real is that sliver of our total selves that exists in the Now. With primitive wisdom ancient tribal people seem to know this intuitively. This is why they find role-taking easy and their self-portraits have so little content. Developing intelligence and self-consciousness has vastly enriched our minds and expanded our knowledge and technical expertise. In the process, however, we have lost the ease of adjustment found in simpler cultures. At a higher point on the evolutionary spiral we have to learn again to live in the Now to enact un-self-consciously the roles most appropriate to the circumstances in which we find ourselves. When in Africa I was much struck by the speed with which the indigenous people learned European ways. The ability to do this, I am sure, is due to their freedom from false ideas about themselves. Unreal self-portraits are an impediment, especially when we feel that we must act on them consistently.

The suggestion that "wake," or wakefulness, has arisen as a result of survival needs for sustained activity to ensure reproduction and safety is supported by the life cycle of innumerable insects. An innate tendency towards unconsciousness and timeless states is graphically illustrated by Bleibtreu in *The Parable of the Beast* when describing the behavior of the cattle tick. He is distinguishing between the real environment and the perceptual world of creatures. The cattle tick requires mammalian blood to set its reproductive cycle in motion. It has been known to wait up to eighteen years in a state of suspended animation for the scent of butyric acid in animal sweat. This is the only signal that will rouse it to action, for it signifies the presence of a warm-blooded animal. At the smell of sweat the tick leaps in the direction from which the smell comes. If it lands on something warm and draws blood, sperm and ovum fuse and the creature starts to live out the rest of its brief life. If it does not, it drops off and finds its way laboriously up another bush; its metabolism slows down, and its short period of wakefulness is replaced by sleep for yet another timeless period.

If we assume that organisms have emerged through life cycles polarized between rest and activity and that activity has become associated first with awareness and then with self-awareness, we can do this quite happily within the current linear theory of evolution. Such a theory leaves open, too, the possibility of further advances in consciousness, since neurophysiologists estimate that ninety percent of the cortex is underdeveloped. However, what can we make of the entity that takes over from Dr. Raikov during artificial reincarnation? It can clearly tap potentials unavailable to the ego self, since the development of new skills means opening up new nerve pathways as well as deepening existing ones. To become a professional artist in twenty-five lessons would normally be impossible for someone with established modes of thought who has never taken any interest in art and cannot draw. Just what takes over from Dr. Raikov and where in the name of Darwinian evolution did it learn its job? Or did it learn it? Do we have to rethink evolutionary theory along with everything else? Do we have to go back to the Greeks again in search of something akin to Aristotle's *entelechy*, some entity of a higher order already in man and guiding his evolution from within, a final cause activating the unfolding of one faculty after another in the world of efficient causes and linear time?

Dr. Raikov has clearly brought us to a frontier, and one can only be relieved that it is something in the subject and not in the hypnotist that takes control and develops latent talents in artificial reincarnation. One would like to feel more sure than one does at present that it can also reject hypnotic suggestion if an unscrupulous hypnotist tried to incarnate, say, a Hitler rather than an Einstein. I have a feeling that perhaps it can, but much more work needs to be done to discover what entity or entities are invoked by this technique and perhaps also by the sort of autosuggestion described in the literature concerning Edgar Cayce. Soviet scientists say that it is not easy to induce the Raikov type of role-taking and that Raikov himself is not always successful. At this stage of the proceedings I think that this is probably a good thing.

The frontier that Raikov has brought science to may be one that some of us have approached from other angles. It is surely no other than the frontier between two levels of ourselves, two centers of direction that probably interact more often than we are aware and the difference between which has never really been scientifically explored. I came to the edge of this frontier as the result of an accident, and the incident has influenced my ideas about the role of unconscious processes in personality theories ever since.

Just before a philosophy examination on an icy winter day in Edinburgh I lost my footing at the top of a flight of stone steps and landed on the small of my back. I was so shocked that it never occurred to me not to take the examination. I allowed myself to be led into the examination hall, where I docilely read through the paper and decided which four questions I would answer. The first two I answered in full possession of my faculties. As the small furnace at the base of my spine hotted up, I began to miss on various cortical cylinders but managed to keep more or less in control while answering question number three. By the time I reached number four, however, I was no longer in command at all. All "I" could do was to hang on to the question and as sentences appeared before my mind grab them and write them down one after another until they stopped coming. By that time, of course, I was punch-drunk with shock and had a large lump right across the bottom of my back. The fantastic outcome of this experience was that I not only got a first-class mark for the whole paper but that my highest mark was for the question "I" had not answered at all.

I came to the frontier again thirteen years later as a secondary result of the same accident. When my back was originally x-rayed, a subluxation of my left hip went unnoticed. Over the years I was to become more and more exhausted as my back came under strain from top to bottom. Odd symptoms occurred from time to time in a whole range of misleading places, and the subluxation was not found until a friend persuaded me to go to a healer at a spiritualist center. My parents were theosophists and I was born in India, so I was familiar with theosophical theories, derived from Eastern sources, about an invisible anatomy of man involving auras and *chakras*. I was consequently quite open-minded about the possibility of techniques like the laying on of hands and therapeutic touch. Moreover, I thought a visit would be interesting whether I benefited in health or not. What I did not expect was to be told that I was a healer myself and to be invited to join the staff of the center and prove this for myself.

It seemed to me an experiment worth trying, though I had never been quite happy with the idea of interfering with someone else's magnetic fields. It had always seemed to me that we must be organizers of our own fields in some sense and that illness, as opposed to accidents, suggested malfunction at some organizational level within the personality. Unless the organizer were treated, it therefore seemed likely that any induced changes in a patient's physical fields would be temporary or, if a specific condition were cured permanently, that new symptoms were likely to break out elsewhere. Nevertheless, the opportunity to study healing in a spiritualist setting seemed too good to miss.

One of the healers at the clinic was of the passive type; having initially told me where to stand and direct my hands, he closed his eyes and allowed himself to become a channel of healing from "the other side," leaving me to my own devices. I had not been working with him long when, to my astonishment, I found my hands exhibiting a will of their own. I did not feel in the least "possessed," and no chilly breezes wafted around my feet. I merely found my hands moving over the patient, often a little above. This alarmed me at first because, since this was a spiritualist center where discarnate doctors and guides were ostensibly in charge, we frequently did not know what was actually wrong with our patients. I used to hurry outside to examine their cards to see if my hands had been working in the right place. I began to understand why I had been asked to join the staff, for, with unfailing regularity, they appeared to have been behaving in ways that made medical sense.

Observing this healing activity with as much objectivity as one can bring to such self-examinations, I found the whole business extraordinarily matter-of-fact. One could stop if necessary and continue after interruptions without any sense of being disturbed or impeded. I could find no evidence to support the idea that I had been taken over by some outside entity, nor was there any lowering of the level of consciousness or any feeling of dissociation. My patients seemed to feel better and were often surprised, as I was myself, at the aptness of things I said "out of the blue." The only significant factor shared by this unusual healing experience and that in the examination room was that in both cases I acted efficiently without any help from the thinking and self-directional areas of my brain.

I was, of course, in no state to study myself on the latter occasion but was well able to do so in the healing clinic.

While actually at work, it was as if the center controlling my activity moved into a part of me other than the ego self that ordinarily directs it. That it was a higher control center seemed indicated not only by its ability to scan a wider perceptual field and by its greater knowledge but also by its skillful handling of body movements to produce effects by methods about which I was consciously completely ignorant. To what extent there is oscillation between this center and lower control centers in ordinary life is something it would be useful to know more about. Dr. Raikov has, I think, found one way to reach it and so release into the pool of consciously available skills new ones inherently available but not so far elicited by the life circumstances of his subjects.

If I am right in this and if the neurophysiologists are right in thinking ninety percent of the brain's potential is still relatively unemployed, an interesting thought arises. Which neural mechanisms are associated with this higher control center? Clearly there may be areas less empty than we think as well as areas awaiting development. Moreover, how right are we to assume that the ego-consciousness from which we chiefly operate is the best level from which to plan our lives? Could part of the new renaissance involve rethinking ourselves in such a way as to include in our self-portraits the idea that we may be junior partners in a larger concern than we have, qua scientists, so far conceived to exist? And may not the direction of the universe be of a similarly complex kind?

I have never been convinced by theories of randomness, and it has always seemed to me that the second law of thermodynamics was one of limited applicability. The universe is orderly on too many levels to be the product of chance mutations and the evolution of species as purely physical events. Far from suggesting a progress towards chaos, the more holistically one looks at the universe, the more it seems to operate under an overall law of synthesis. It is true that individual structures disintegrate, be they molecules or men. A Heraclitean flux is part of the nature of things, but as obvious as the death of one structured field is the simultaneous birth of others. Similarly, over the long history of the planet, though species have died out, new and more advanced manifestations of life have emerged to take their place. Order is everywhere and of so functional a character as to suggest that, behind so much constructive organization, there must be purpose of some kind, however difficult to define or to prove.

The peoples of antiquity, observing the cyclical regularity of the seasons and the patterned diversity of nature, invented gods and spirits as principles of control responsible for the natural order. There is no tribe so far known to anthropology that does not have its creator and creation myth. Are we more right in regarding the creator concept as out of date? And are we the better for it? Wearing my scientific hat, I am not prepared to arbitrate but only to say that, on the evidence, it is as much an assertion of faith to dismiss a creator as to assume one. The only rational position is agnostic. The more we probe the secrets of the universe, however, the more difficult it is to avoid the impression of purposive forces at work, guiding us through an evolutionary process in which a balance between species, environments, and energies has, until man began interfering, been continuously and subtly maintained. In nature the forces of entropy and negentropy seem to coexist in harmonious interaction, and, before man put himself in charge, it entered no one's head that our planet would die of anything but old age.

I wonder if a higher control center, such as Raikov and Edgar Cayce seem to have activated and the presence of which I sensed when healing, is operating in all of us but that our awareness of it is blocked by the extra cortical activity necessary for the development of intellect and self-consciousness. It is possible that it is not something latent or dormant so much as something overlooked, at least by those who belong to the privileged twenty percent with above-average intelligence. Perhaps we should be more humble before nature and the man in the street in this matter also. The average person may be guided by emotional and practical considerations but also by instinctive responses that are prompted by the higher control center that can see what sense perception misses and reason fails to spot; the center that is also able to use the body with the intelligence and economy of a master crafter.

The way in which the two levels of the self interact in high-grade creative work is graphically revealed in *The Double Helix*, James D. Watson's autobiographical account of the discovery of the molecular structure of DNA. It is also a lively tale about the rivalry between scientists working in the same field and the different attitudes they display, ranging from a respect for fair play in trespassing on one another's preserves to cutthroat competition with no holds barred.

Watson was a keen, young American postgraduate student with a strong interest in genes and a hunch about DNA (deoxyribonucleic acid). This gene is a very special and complex molecule that carries the chromosomes responsible for passing on hereditary characteristics. At the time, the early 1950s, biochemists were chiefly concerned to unravel the structure of proteins, though O. T. Avery at the Rockefeller Institute had shown that hereditary traits could be transmitted from one bacterial cell to another by purified DNA molecules alone. Watson's hunch was that DNA and not protein was the key to the hereditary role of the gene. By great good fortune and not a little wangling he managed to find his way into the Cavendish Laboratories in Cambridge, England, and into the company of Francis Crick, who shared his views on the role of DNA.

At that time Crick was thirty-five. Originally a physicist, he turned biologist after reading *What is Life?* by the eminent physicist Erwin Schrödinger. In this book Schrödinger highlighted the gene as the key component of living cells. Crick was not only brilliant; he was an extremely versatile and lively theoretician and, as Watson found, "fun to talk to." Prior to Watson's arrival in Cambridge, however, Crick had only thought sporadically about

DNA and its role in heredity. He was, moreover, reluctant to concentrate on it on grounds of fair play, since another Englishman, Maurice Wilkins, was already working on it through x-ray diffraction, the method in general use for studying the constitution of molecules. He was, however, spurred to investigate its genetic role by learning that Linus Pauling of the California Institute of Technology was becoming interested. Pauling was another colorful character, an ingenious researcher and first-class showman. It was he who first demonstrated the helical element in the structure of protein by the use of a model made up of colored balls representing the constituent atoms. Having gone so far with the protein part of the gene, it would not be long before he turned his attention to DNA.

A transatlantic battle was joined, and the race was on to see who could crack the structure of DNA first. The two English universities, with Crick and Watson at Cambridge and Maurice Wilson and his brilliant associate, Rosalind Franklin, in London, combined forces, albeit not always so happily as they might. Wilkins and Franklin concentrated on x-ray crystallography, while Crick and Watson took a leaf out of Pauling's book and worked with models. As Watson writes, the essential trick was "to ask which atoms like to sit next to each other." They decided that the best way to get answers was to construct models and play with them, like a child with colored shapes. This method of dealing with atomic models is now general, as many a television science program shows. Then, however, it was new and played an important part in leading Crick and Watson to what was probably the most fruitful discovery of this century, one that opened up the entire field of genetic engineering and man-made substances.

Reading Watson's account, one gets the feeling that manipulating the physical models, combining the use of mind and hands, contributed very significantly in bringing these two inventive men to their final insight. It is as if there were oscillation between a center in the brain mediating reasoning and a "hunch" center in all original thought and between a hunch center and cerebral areas controlling sensory-motor responses in skilled craftwork. The trick is, as Watson might say, to make all three areas work together. I know myself that my ideas flow more freely if I write with my pen in my hand than if I merely press buttons and a machine does the work for me. My mind seems to like the cooperation of my hands. However, in the examination room and the healing clinic my thinking mind was in abeyance. Under certain circumstances intellectual tasks can apparently be performed as automatically as a skilled knitter can work a complicated pattern. The exercise of unusual skills has to be willed but does not necessarily need the cooperation of the reasoning mind.

When I found my hands functioning independently of my conscious direction in the healing situation, I was of course aware that I could be the victim of some form of morbid dissociation. In view of my chronic state of exhaustion at the time, it was all too likely. However, I could discover no evidence of it and the appropriateness of my activities there, as in the examination room, suggested that they were governed by objective considerations and not by my subjective state. Nevertheless, one must beware of the assumption that entities or aspects of oneself that take over in all types of dissociated state are of a superior order. Psychological textbooks are full of instances that show that this is not so. Cases of possession and split personality can produce most unsavory characters. In ordinary life loss of self-control can bring onto the stage aspects of ourselves of which we are thoroughly ashamed but which can take us over nonetheless. It is clear that parts of ourselves that are able to control the way our bodies behave can be of many different kinds. The idea of the self as a collection of subpersonalities capable of using the physical body suggests that the Hindus may be more right than Western scientists in believing the body to be a passive principle upon which other aspects of the personality act in terms of their own needs and purposes. This, however, does not make it any easier to explain how subpersonalities, let alone a subliminal Self at a higher level, can use it.

That we are ultimately the organizers of our own energy fields seems confirmed by the fact that there seems to be in us some part that resists intrusions that militate against individuality and wholeness. This is not only exemplified by the refusal of hypnotic subjects to perform acts that violate deeply held values; it is built into the body's immune system. In the present enthusiasm for transplant surgery too little attention is being paid to the implications of resistance. The phenomenon of resistance in immunology is not contrived by nature just to make transplant surgery more difficult or to prevent immoral hypnotists from corrupting worthy citizens. For some reason human individuality is so important that the evolutionary process has fostered and protected it even to the point of preferring the death of the body to the acceptance of alien organs that might prolong its existence. Surely this tells us something quite surprising about our so-called material universe, for it clearly implies that nature, left to itself, prizes individuality more highly than mere physical survival.

5
Science and Experience

*T*he higher control center can hardly be identified with any part of the body it controls, since it must work through the finer fields with which the body appears to be associated. It must, however, have its physiological anchorage points, and finding these mechanisms is essential if we are to understand the human being as a complex system of interlocking fields that function as a single whole. It is as much a mistake in any holistic approach to concentrate on selves and overlook the mechanisms through which they relate to the material world as to concentrate on the mechanisms without reference to the selves whose ends they serve. As scientists we need to analyze ourselves as persons in order to better understand consciousness. Equally, we need to analyze our bodily organization both in order to operate it more effectively and to repair it more wisely when it breaks down. Science in the new renaissance must treat human beings as wholes whether we think about them in terms of sources, fields, and chemical structures or in terms of body, mind, and spirit.

There is another point that must be emphasized if we are to deal adequately with the reality in which we actually live and not merely with an abstraction, which scientists call the physical universe and treat as if it is all there is. It is a false assumption made by both the scientist and the layperson that we perceive objects as they exist apart from us, "out there." This belief has great practical and survival value, but it is simply not true. It is based on a useful illusion contrived for us by the brain to simplify experience and make it more manageable. Nature and evolution have developed the brain not only as a receiver but also as a selector of impulses from the outer world. We do not "recognize" unwanted sensations. If this were not so, perception would not be the effective tool that it is.

It is effective because it is a selective process that patterns incoming stimuli in such a way that they can end up as images in the mind. These images are representations of things, not things as they are in themselves. The philosopher Immanuel Kant pointed this out in the eighteenth century, and it was again stressed at the beginning of the present century by the Austrian philosopher Edmund Husserl. Husserl called his world view *phenomenology*, which is the technical term used by philosophers to refer to the theory that we can only know appearances. We often talk as if phenomena were things that exist as realities in the external world. By derivation, however, the word "phenomenon" comes from the Greek *phainomenon*, meaning appearance. Phenomenology, therefore, is the study of the world as it appears to be—in other words, the world as we experience it, as perception presents it to our minds. Husserl believed that this was the only world that we can know directly.

His ideas gave birth to an important school of psychology, the Gestalt school. This school made a special study of the mechanisms by means of which we see things as meaningful wholes. (A *gestalt* is a whole.) What we know is determined by our modes of perception and the range of stimuli from the outside world to which our senses can respond. It is perception that conditions our experience, and the interpretations that we put on our perceptions that determine our behavior. Perception produces the patterns that integrate the sensations received by our various sense organs into meaningful wholes.

How these wholes become meaningful is another question and a difficult one. Moreover it is one that must be tackled in depth if it is to be answered satisfactorily. It is much more likely to be answered satisfactorily from the standpoint of the psychologist through field theories than through mind-brain dualism, which most scientists tend to presuppose. The concerted efforts of psychologists and physiologists are required if we are to arrive at theories of human beings as gestalts in which body and mind work together to produce experience.

Western science truncates itself when it overlooks the implications of phenomenology and Gestalt psychology. When, for instance, scientists locate the center of consciousness in the brain, they oversimplify a complex situation. The cerebral cortex contains a mass of signals about the external environment picked up by peripheral nerves, which are then encoded and relayed to the brain. What is in the brain is not the images and ideas that make up our actual experience of things. Somewhere between the energy fields of the body and its organs must lie fields of consciousness associated with some superphysical part of our communication system, which converts signals from "out there" into percepts and concepts "in here."

It is because we fail to recognize that the communication system between the outside world and the conscious self, the witness and interpretor of events, has other levels than the physical that we get stuck in the brain-mind dilemma. (Nor does our addiction to scientific materialism help.) All our experience indicates that we are selves living in perceptual worlds made up of recognizable feelings and significant images. This is the environment that we actually experience. The world of our bodies is a world of signals, which it takes all our scientific ingenuity to decode. We cannot experience these signals directly any more than we can know directly the objects around us. Earache, for example, as experienced is simply a painful feeling. Its physiology, however, is something quite different and more complex. It is vital to the understanding of our experience of earache but not a part of it. Understanding the causes of earache and enduring earache are two distinct and widely differing experiences.

Perhaps one of the most useful modern versions of phenomenology that I have come across is that of William Arkle as expounded in his book *A*

Geography of Consciousness. It is useful because it can be integrated into science more readily than most. Though a mystic and visionary who developed his ideas by exploring his own consciousness, he started out as an engineer and used his skills in the British navy in World War II. After the war he studied art but discontinued his college course after two years. Having discovered mysticism and esotericism, he wanted to develop his own approach to painting and use meditation to understand and refine his nature. His inner explorations seem to have involved a combination of rigorous self-observation and painting his visionary experiences to help capture their significance. In his book he gives an account of the theories to which his experiences brought him, and it is here that his scientific training as an engineer shows.

His exposition, whose province is the entire field of consciousness, is couched in the language of communications theory. He talks about consciousness as a communications network and analyzes experience in terms of vectors. He sees attitudes as filters that strain out certain aspects of the environment and permit others to pass. Values and social conditioning play crucial parts in the development of the filters, which, consciously or unconsciously, determine the nature of the experiences we actually have.

According to Arkle, there are three vectors, V1, V2, and V3. The first is the carrier of consciousness as something that can be structured and organized into recognizable images and ideas. It enables consciousness to be executive and practical and to concentrate attention on the events that it experiences. The second has to do with the range and quality of consciousness. It diffuses it and unifies it at the same time by bringing it in touch with events on an ever-widening scale but at the same time holding its contents together. If we are lacking in V1, we tend to communicate badly and manipulate our inner resources clumsily. If we are short on V2, our field of consciousness tends to be narrow and we do not generate strong incentives or give V1 enough material to work with. Someone strong on V1 but weak on V2 could be very narrow-minded but highly competent. Someone strong on V2 but weak on V1 could have many good ideas but be unable to apply them successfully. V3 relates to attitudes and the series of filters through which we evaluate experience. Values and the attitudes they generate are seen as shifting along a scale from naked self-interest and survival to the serenity that accompanies high ideals and inner harmony. We all tend to have a basic attitude which colors the value that we place upon all our experiences and upon the way we react when communicating with other people. It filters our self-judgments. Whether we are conscious of it or not, our experience is constantly being filtered in this way, and the resulting states of consciousness that arise in us constitute the environment in which we actually live.

Arkle goes on from this analysis to argue that the physical world is only important to us as a medium through which we receive and transmit communications. Moreover, these communications are first and foremost descriptions of states of consciousness and only secondarily the statements of fact that we

assume them to be. This is because our consciousness is primarily concerned with filters—our own
and other people's. Its aim is to improve on the
quality of its own attitudes. Other people's attitudes
are important because they help us to modify and
correct our own. Arkle says that we only lose sight
of this fact about ourselves because our intercom-
munications are themselves so interesting that they
distract us from our chief concern, which is to become more comfortable in and with ourselves.

He then deals with what he calls "real being,"
or absolute consciousness and absolute identity.
This he treats as transcendental in the sense that
it cannot become an object of direct experience, a
phenomenon. It nevertheless runs the show. Sometimes the phenomenal, conscious self knows this,
as I did in the healing situation; more often it does
not.

Our real being is what Arkle calls our first-order
filter. Our second-order filter is the conscious self
in a state of detachment and self-observation. Our
physical personality is our third-order filter. Most
people tend to identify with their third-order filter,
but it is important, according to Arkle, that, if we
are to lift the world out of the morass of materialism
into which it has sunk, as many people as possible
work to attain a higher consciousness—clean up
their filters, so to speak. Civilization requires that
more of us operate at the second-order level from
which we can occasionally sense the presence of
our real being with its gifts of serenity and a wider
vision of what our world as experienced might
become.

Arkle contends that the physical environment should be regarded as a communication medium through which signals pass back and forth between the individual and his or her surroundings. He points out that, while we know a great deal about how encoded replicas of events reach the brain from the sense organs and about the relation between certain cerebral events and specific experiences, our knowledge tends to stop there. Nevertheless, it seems only logical to assume that there must be some supplementary system that transmits information from the brain to consciousness. In other words, there must be intermediate energy fields of some sort. He suggests that it is because consciousness and this part of the communication network are so intangible that science keeps trying to find a mechanistic theory to explain them. As a result, it tends not to distinguish clearly between the functions of consciousness and the functions of its channels of communication. Each needs to be seen as playing a separate role in the overall functioning of the individual as a person. It is because imbalances have resulted from our rapid technological advances along V1 without a corresponding expansion of our range along V2 that science has become so inhibited and narrow.

If we do indeed make the distinction he advocates and attend to our own experience, we can confirm that, as selves, we are relatively remote from our body and physical personality and also that the space-time continuum in which physical events occur has no direct bearing on conditions within consciousness itself. An instance of this is the different orders of space-time within which a writer's consciousness is moving when imagining, planning, rationalizing, or remembering in connection with his or her work and that in which the hand is conveying pen to paper.

Arkle is also quite right in pointing out that the inner attitudes we adopt act as filters in consciousness between the center of awareness and what is going on in the external world. They modify how the environment is experienced irrespective of which signals are being received from outside. They can also seriously distort them, predisposing us to biased or misguided judgments. These must take place at the level of interpretation and so in superneural parts of the communications network. From this assumption Arkle goes on to suggest that only some more ethereal form of matter can continue the process of transmission from the brain to the individual's center of awareness. There must be some superphysical part of the system into which electronic signals from the nervous system can be transposed. Postulating such a network would be compatible with Vasiliev's contention that his thought fields are material if "material" is not defined in a limited sense. It is also compatible with our experience of multiple bodies, as Arkle himself realized when proposing his concept of bodies of communication.

As we have seen, Arkle developed his ideas not in a theosophical or yogic context but in one of communications theory. He regarded matter as first and foremost communication and only secondarily as a structure of energy. In other words, every material object expresses something and so is constructed as an information system. This is why he speaks

of matter-consciousness and why he stresses the
need to be openminded when defining consciousness, since even nonliving entities behave in a way
that suggests both a specific role in nature and a
responsiveness to the environment while fulfilling
it. This is true even of atomic particles.

The idea that subatomic particles may play a part
in mediating consciousness is not new. It was postulated by Annie Besant and C. W. Leadbeater in
Occult Chemistry in connection with an entity they
called "the ultimate physical atom." The origin of
Occult Chemistry goes back to 1895 when the
authors began a clairvoyant study of the atoms of
all the chemical elements. It was in the ultimate
physical atom, however, that they claimed to see
physical energies intermingling with finer energies
from "astral" levels associated with consciousness.
I have myself envisaged the possibility that fundamental particles at the interface between mind and
matter might operate like screws winding and un-
winding to let thought descend or sense impressions rise, depending on the direction of their spins
(*Kundalini in the Physical World*). Arkle saw the
need to relate consciousness to types of matter even
finer than the fundamental particles of physics. As
he writes, it is arbitrary to assume that other levels
do not exist merely because they are currently beyond our powers of observation.

By conceiving matter-consciousness as evolving
into a form of matter that he calls "matter-self-consciousness" he sees the self at the center of bodies
of communication of varying material densities and
conscious sensitivities. These bodies also operate
as filters of experience each at its own level. This

would give the mobile center of consciousness (with which one identifies), the capacity to range through all the levels on which an evolving self is currently able to function. Here we have a theory of bodies associated with an evolutionary theory of consciousness. It complements existing theories of the evolution of species because it suggests that, even if the human body has developed as far as animal bodies can evolve, the evolutionary process need not come to a full stop. It can proceed by elaborating and modifying our higher bodies of communication, producing even more effective and responsive fields at higher energy frequencies. In this way consciousness can be both widened and deepened. If what we are told about the underused areas of the brain is correct, this could be achieved without any radical changes in physical structure. It would be merely a matter of the evolutionary process turning inward, evolution of form giving place to evolution of consciousness.

Once one recognizes that the human universe has two dimensions along which it can be scientifically explored, that of the environment perceived and that of ourselves as perceiving subjects, it becomes obvious that we need to devise new models for research, based on new ways of seeing both ourselves and the universe. The problem of finding new ways of looking at the universe will be easier to solve than the problem that we ourselves present to potential model-makers. As far as the environment is concerned, the primary need is for scientists and philosophers to stop regarding life and mind as intrusions into the physical world and accept them as natives who have been occupying it all the time without being recognized for what they are. Where we ourselves are concerned, the situation is more complex. The measure of objectivity that we can maintain when looking out to the environment is harder to achieve when we study ourselves. This is not only because it is like asking a diagnostic machine to analyze itself; it is also because, as we have seen, we do not yet know the scope and nature of the machinery that we have at our disposal. For this reason now is the time for science to turn its attention away from making ever more ingenious artifacts with which to investigate the physical world and begin to consider more seriously the potential of human bodies as exploratory tools.

It is also important that scientists should not adopt dismissive attitudes towards unorthodox thinkers, scorning as "mere speculation" the offerings of philosophers struggling with the mind-body dichotomy and psychologists trying to explain psychics and psychic phenomena. All scientific discoveries, as well as the creative resynthesis of material already discovered, are the end products of speculation. Only the most pedestrian scientific chores can be carried on without it. To speculate is to wonder about something, and wonder and curiosity are the two most important gifts in the innovator's armory of available talents. A feeling for what fits is also valuable, as is the recognition, often unconscious, that what once fitted the needs of the past no longer meets the needs of the present. A sense of what fits where is as useful in integrating new insights into an existing body of knowledge as it is in combining shapes in order to complete a jigsaw puzzle.

When building complex models, whether materially or mentally, fitness demands that nothing that is essential be left out. To build a model of a human being or a human universe is so complicated that it is not surprising that science has shrunk from tackling either. If we are to meet the challenges of nature and our own times, however, we must make the attempt. Without it there can be no new renaissance. Even if we make mistakes—and we shall —they can generate new approaches and spotlight new directions in which to look.

A difficulty that will confront many of us will be the confusion of two frames of reference. For instance, as both a philosopher and a psychologist I know that what lies "out there" is only contacted at one remove and that the perceptual worlds of creatures can differ widely. As a person I tend, as we all do, to take the view that what I perceive is what is actually there. The difference between certitude and truth is easily overlooked in the practical business of living. This is because convenient habits of perception filter out impressions that can complicate life unnecessarily. Too much "truth" can be a handicap rather than a help in everyday life, and too much insight into ourselves can be paralyzing at times. It is healthier to oscillate between both attitudes, provided that we know what we are doing and do not see them in inappropriate ways when it matters. Action can be "sicklied o'er with the pale cast of thought," but thought can be "sicklied o'er" if we bring to it attitudes that belong in the world of action.

Materialism and the unresolved body-mind dilemma have combined to restrict science to the denser levels of the phenomenal world. Specialization and the development of disciplines in relative isolation from one another still tend to prevent science from advancing on a united front. All these factors operate against breadth of view and a common frame of reference. Science badly needs an integrating philosophy that will counteract its further fragmentation. This is all the more true since the business of explaining life, which once devolved upon priests, is increasingly being regarded as a matter for scientists. If religion is to stage a comeback, it can only now do so with the blessing of science. However, the corollary is also true. If science is to replace religion, it must be able to address itself to the whole person. It must be prepared to tackle the universe as a complex human experience and not pick away at it piecemeal.

If we are to know the world as it really is, we must also throw overboard limiting stereotypes about what we can and cannot do. We must probe our own frontiers as well as those of the universe. We need to stand before the human body and its powers with an open mind. If we tell a child often enough that he is stupid, he becomes stupid. Similarly, if we believe that we can respond only to a narrow range of stimuli, we condition ourselves to these limitations. It is likely that we can do far more with the help of our bodies if we put half the faith in them that we put in our machines.

6
Perception and the Perceiver

*T*he concept of interrelated energy fields or bodies of communication fits better with the idea of an integrated personality than one in which body and mind are placed in two separate realities. If, however, the bodies of communication are interpenetrating sheaths, as clairvoyant reports suggest and yogis contend, there must be mechanisms at the interfaces between sheaths capable of transposing the energies of higher systems so that they can be adapted for use in lower systems, and vice versa. For instance, what happened when Phoebe Bendit switched from normal vision to probe a patient's body with what she called "etheric vision" and others sometimes called her "x-ray eyes"?

That she was not using x-rays seems clear, since what she saw did not resemble x-ray photographs but the counterparts of inner organs, entire and functioning. It would seem more likely that beyond the electrochemical levels of the sensory nervous system are others mediating vision but capable of deeper penetration and wider scanning powers. Such wider scanning powers of the body I had myself already experienced when healing; where my experience differed from Mrs. Bendit's lay in her ability to move her mobile center of consciousness to a level that mine could not reach. A part of me registered what Mrs. Bendit described in visual terms, but my conscious self was not able to identify with it sufficiently to do the same.

There seems no reason to doubt that every human body, as a multidimensional but integrated system, has the potential to transform ordinary vision into clairvoyant vision through a series of energy exchanges. Normally, as we know, changes in experience are accompanied by changes in the way a variety of forces behave in the body. If, in the course of our individual development, our experiential capability enlarges, there is no reason to suppose that this functional correlation ceases to hold. It does, however, suggest that previously little-used energy fields will become more active and the range of frequencies to which the body can respond become increasingly extended. The fact that conscious experience and the mechanisms that mediate it are correlative, changing in phase with each other, should dispose of the mind-body problem, because all experiences, like earache, can either be analyzed as events in consciousness or as events in the mechanisms that subserve it.

This correlation reinforces the need to pursue research along two dimensions, that of the environment as a perceptual phenomenon of an extremely complex kind and that of human beings as the conscious perceivers of it. The body as an object of scientific investigation is part of the world perceived as "out there." Our inner experiences as objects of study are parts of an environment "in here." The center of individual awareness, qua perceiving subject, is distinct from both and even more remote from the machinery that converts signals from the world outside into the objects of experience as they appear in consciousness. However, to do justice to both environment within and external world without, we need to offer to the perceiving subject in ourselves a new perspective on both. We need a more phenomenological and wider-ranging approach to the psychology of inner experience and also to the biology and cosmology of the world of objects that appears to lie outside us.

An illustration of work that is developing along these lines was shown on a television program called "Broken Images," which dealt with two cases of visual agnosia. Agnosia is a perceptual disorder that destroys the ability to recognize familiar objects as meaningful wholes while leaving intact both the memory of events and the capacity to recognize the constituent parts of things. Two cases were used to illustrate both the patients' difficulties in making sense of their surroundings and the medical psychologist's difficulties in analyzing exactly where the perceptual process had broken down. One patient, an Englishman called John, had been the victim of a slight stroke from which he had otherwise recovered. The other, an American called Larry, had been in a motorcycle accident in which he had also lost the use of an arm. Both were intelligent and articulate men, which made them ideal subjects for research.

For the most part the psychologists concentrated on the perceptual experiences of the two men. For instance, both could describe in great detail the various parts of faces, including their own, without being able to recognize to whom they belonged. They seemed unable to make the transition from a collection of parts to a significant whole. Larry could not recognize himself in a mirror until he walked into it, and John could not recognize his wife until she started to speak. It was not only the gestalt element, the combining of related parts in the visual field, that was defective: both subjects had to reason from an analysis of the parts into what categories things should be placed. For example, shown a photograph of a Christmas tree in his sitting room, John puzzled out what the central complex of shapes and colors might be. Deciding that it was a shrub of some sort, he presumed that the door and window must be on the outside of a house. The more he reasoned, the further he became removed from the scene depicted in the photograph. Similarly, viewing the Houses of Parliament from a riverboat on the Thames, he was completely unable to place it. He thought that the tower might be a warehouse until his attention was drawn to the white circular shape at the top. This, he decided, might be a clock but at no time did he recognize it as Big Ben. On the other hand, his memory of the topography of a friend's house was exact, though he realized that he would be quite unable to find his way around if he actually went there.

The psychologists tried an experiment to learn whether either had any knowledge at other levels of consciousness of objects that were not recognized consciously. Here they found that John and Larry differed. At the time of the Cuban missile crisis, when presented with a picture of Fidel Castro, Larry did not recognize him; a lie-detector type of machine, revealed that part of him reacted to Castro even while he was denying all knowledge of him. On the other hand, John's body did not react at all to either familiar or strange faces.

There may be some relation between the subconscious recognition process in Larry and the unconscious knowledge that I displayed when healing. It is possible that Phoebe Bendit had conscious clairvoyant capability, while my own operated below the threshold of awareness. This might explain an odd experience that I once had with a medium. Her guide asserted that I was psychic and, when I denied this, said that my gift lay in being able to read "the invisible images." This may be true, for later when I was using patients' paintings diagnostically, I found that images seemed to convey more to me than to the painters themselves, though they readily accepted the relevance of most of my interpretations when we discussed them.

Behind this sort of "penetration" into things may lie unconscious perceptual processes of a clairvoyant order. If so, they may be exercised in ordinary life far more widely than we realize. Agnosic people like Larry might be good subjects for the kind of training in ESP undertaken by parapsychologists using hypnosis and biofeedback and might be able to learn to use clairvoyance to make up for the deficiencies of their ordinary vision.

Colin Blakemore, a professor of physiology at the University of Oxford, hosted the television program.

His final comments were interesting from a phenomenological point of view: he pointed out that
much of what we perceive is a construction of our
own making. We can readily confirm this for ourselves. We do not know a table as a table until we
have learned the word and experienced a variety
of objects that we finally come to recognize instantly
as tables. As Professor Blakemore also indicated,
there is a great deal of social conditioning implicit
in perception, both in what we see and how we see
it.

Science is properly an attempt to give a rational
description of the known world using empirical
verification as a corrective to flights of fancy, and
experimental methods whenever the subject matter permits and our ingenuity is equal to the task.
It is, therefore, as the phenomenological approach
makes increasingly clear, essentially unscientific
to dismiss any phenomenon as nonexistent merely because it lies outside our personal experience,
eludes experimental manipulation, or cannot be
confirmed by a reputable third party. If I have a vision while alone on a desert island, my problem is
to decide whether I have had a hallucination, a
clairvoyant episode, or a dream. I would be merely foolish if I tried to convince myself that I had experienced nothing at all. It is equally irrational for
scientists to decry the value of subjective evidence
while resting their claim to objectivity on that ob-
tained through the five senses. As we have seen,
perception itself is a subjective experience. In the
last analysis both the inner world that we call "subjective" and the outer world that we call "objective" are body-based psychic constructs. The

difference between the two lies not in one being more real than the other but in one being more directly experienced than the other. Both raise the same problems: how to interpret the data and how to communicate our findings.

The fact that our experience must be interpreted and that this is as true of sense-based as of intuitive-psychic events can be demonstrated from within science itself. One can think of two examples. One concerns the difficulties scientists underwent in interpreting the data of electron microscopy before they arrived at a shared set of visual images that could be used as a basis for communication. The process must have been very similar to that by which a child learns its mother tongue. Groups of purely subjective happenings are found to be shared and to have word labels that, if appropriately affixed, enable one to verify the sharing. A new vocabulary has developed out of the marriage of electron microscopy and computer technology. It has done so because imagery has been extended to include new reaches of the environment within the known-to-be-shared physical world that we call objective. Objective reality is only that part of subjective reality that we experience as separate from us and know to be shared.

Another example of the extent to which sense-data need to be interpreted and of how much of their objectivity is based on shared language can be found in fundamental physics. What has been actually perceived is infinitesimal compared with the amount that has been inferred and come to be shared through the development of a common vocabulary. It is quite astonishing how quickly a quark has become more real than a hunch to the scientific establishment, even a hunch that proves to be right, and how much more readily a diagnosis made by a scanning machine will be accepted than one based on clairvoyant vision. Yet, as experiences, hunches are common and second sight has been with humanity for centuries.

Scientists and doctors tend to be more hampered than they realize when it comes to interpretation. They are inclined to assume that their training enables them to differentiate between the real and the imaginary without realizing that their judgments are necessarily professionally conditioned. When dismissive attitudes are allowed to creep into one's training, one needs to be wary about the presuppositions on which they are based. Dismissive biases of which one is unaware can put the probing mind into a straitjacket so comfortable that one does not even recognize it for what it is. Excluding life and mind from the physical universe, for instance, immediately makes their presence in the experiential world something that science has to explain. They can no longer be seen as inherent energies native to certain species but become problems that are all the more intractable because they should not be problems at all.

Another way in which we tend to reduce the scope of the phenomenal world is by generalizing from our own experience. In interpreting our environment, whether material or social, there is a natural tendency to assume that others see things as we do. A color blind person who learns to use color words appropriately may never know that his subjective imagery is defective. Those with good sight and hearing are inclined to be clumsy with the blind and impatient with the deaf. The intelligent and the mentally robust readily assume that the less intelligent and the emotionally unstable could do better if they tried. Religion is easily dismissed as escapism if one has never had a religious experience of any depth.

This generalizing tendency obscures the fact that the phenomenal world is only a segment of the surrounding physical environment. It is probably associated with the way in which the sense organs evolved as aids to survival. With primitive animals it is vital to be able to recognize prey and to distinguish friend from foe. In the case of the frog, for example, an approaching fly is seen so that it may be caught; a receding fly fails to register. All frogs react in the same manner and, if they could think, no doubt would assume that all frogs see flies in that way because that is the way that the world is made. Sensory information systems in creatures have become increasingly complex in the course of evolution, and in the case of man language and self-consciousness have enormously enlarged the range of responses open to individuals within the species. This is why generalizing from one's own experience simplifies life but at the expense of contracting one's environment and blunting one's sensitivity to individual differences and the sensory possibilities of the body. This is as true for scientists as for the rest of us.

The work of zoologists has done most to open our eyes to these facts, and it is becoming increasingly clear that there are as many physical worlds as there are species making their different selections out of the total environment. The hawk's eye sees naturally where a man would need binoculars. The African knife fish takes its bearings from the distortions in an electric field that it creates itself in a world that it can barely see and in water that it scarcely feels. Its world is quite different from that of the pressure-sensitive fishes.

Animal bodies are capable of a vast range of responses in a wide variety of environments, and organs from earlier stages of evolution regularly appear during the embryonic development of later ones. This is very noticeable in the human fetus, so it is too early to assume that mankind cannot exercise the skills that we take for granted in other creatures. It is also too early to classify any form of perception as extrasensory. We may yet uncover physiological mechanisms that people with unusual gifts manipulate unconsciously but that become available to conscious manipulation through techniques such as biofeedback, for example. It is possible that what we call "extrasensory" is merely not yet scientifically detectable or explicable to the rational modern mind.

Work on vision is constantly bringing home to us the fact that mind, as well as life, is inherent in nature as we know it. The idea that the eye is a camera is quite false. Its recording is sketchy, with much blurring at the edges. The area of clear focus, the fovea centralis, is very small. Psychophysiologists have shown that the parts of the nervous system that subserve imagination play a far greater role in constructing the perceptual world than does the eye itself. Indeed, so strong are the image-building forces that some embryologists wonder whether there may not be some sort of blueprint of the environment encoded in our genes and carried over from generation to generation. Any such coded information would not of itself be a picture, an outline diagram presented to consciousness. The dense body's role is to provide the electrochemical substrate of mental processes, not to take the mind's place as the controller of those energy fields responsible for mediating images and ideas.

One area of interaction between imagination and the nervous system has been uncovered by M. E. and A. B. Scheibel, a medical husband-and-wife team, one a psychiatrist and the other a neuroanatomist. They investigated the relation between hallucinations and movements in the very fine fibers of the reticular nervous complexes in the brain stem and discovered that there is a correlation between the presence of imagery before the mind and minute changes in the arrangement of the fibers. Just as events in the auditory nerves accompany our experience of earache, so, apparently, do events in the reticular nervous system accompany our experience of imagery. Indeed, it is possible that, as the eye keeps objects in focus by rapid movements too small to be detected, infinitely fine changes in the nervous system may hold the image of the environment steady in our minds in spite of the endless flux of impressions that impinge on it.

Another discovery that suggests that mind and body work as a unit is the effect of personality on the priorities given to different parts of the perceptual field. Unconscious biases influence judgment and are another reason why claims of objectivity in science must be necessarily relative. Norman A. Witkin conducted an interesting series of experiments that showed that there is a "personality constant" that determines even the way in which we straighten a crooked picture. At the beginning of his investigation his object was to study to what extent test subjects used clues from the visual field or the body's gravity sense when orientating themselves in relation to the upright. His findings and their implications are sufficiently relevant to our discussion to be considered at some length.

In order to confuse the sense of balance, he contrived a small room with the fourth side missing. Across this, affixed to a bar, was a chair into which the subjects were strapped. Both chair and room could be rotated independently. After both had been tilted in the dark, the light was turned on, and the experimenter adjusted and readjusted the chair until the subjects felt that they were sitting upright. So dependent were some on visual clues that they claimed to feel upright even at fifty-two degrees off true. If these same subjects shut their eyes so that the body came into play, the upright posture was accurately recognized.

What interested Witkin was that, while there was wide variation between one subject and another, the same subject showed a constant degree of deviation from the upright. This constancy, which extended to all subjects, led Witkin to run a gamut of tests and by a process of elimination to uncover a generally applicable psychological factor. There was a wide spectrum between the extremes of complete dependence on visual clues and complete dependence on the kinesthetic sense. Those least dependent on visual clues were better at problem-solving because they were less distracted by context. They tended to be creative and socially independent but in extreme cases were bad mixers and sometimes antisocial to the point of eccentricity. Children were found to be almost totally dependent on vision until about the age of eight; after that they became increasingly body-dependent until adolescence. From about fourteen, when peer-group mores become important, visual clues were again used more often until the individual arrived at a personal balance between the two ways of evaluating, which thereafter became a personality constant. Women, whose traditional roles tend to require more social awareness, tend to use visual clues more than men, but it is not known whether this is an inherent or adaptive characteristic.

Experiments such as this and research into the sensory apparatus of animals and the psychosomatic reactions of human beings in health and disease show that the physical world open to perception is a far larger and more complex place than we currently assume in framing theories about it. Any body of knowledge that sets out to explain it must recognize that we live in an environmental context only part of which we are ever going to perceive and be prepared to investigate our own capabilities in the same way that zoologists study those of animals. This means questioning orthodox models about our capacities and allowing sufficiently for individual differences in both acuity and range of sensibility. We know that some people have absolute pitch and others do not, that some are acutely sensitive to hues while others are in varying degrees color blind. To a limited extent we accept the possibility of enhancing perceptual sensitivities, but the idea that under certain conditions the human eye may be able to rival the electron microscope is given short shrift as is the possibility that the trained clairvoyant may be able to see fundamental particles. The fact that theoretical physicists have done so intuitively does not seem to have suggested to scientists that clairvoyance may also be a form of perception of the physical world and bear some relation to the way our bodies are made; that it is merely perception of a higher order.

There seem to be two different ways in which perception and imagination work together to create the phenomenal world. One is with the eyes of the dense body and the other is with the eyes of the mind. We can have penetrating insight both of the kind found in electron microscopy and in Mrs. Bendit's investigation of the vital etheric field, in which imagination elaborates percepts produced by focusing attention on a material object. Both microscope and sensitive remain in the ordinary world, with the center of attention moving over limited areas to bring different parts of the field into focus in the usual way. The difference is that the clairvoyant must convey her findings in words, which means that they come to the scientist less directly. However, they do come in a way that is subject to discussion and questioning and may aid interpretation by supplementing the raw data of the electron microscope.

When the eyes of the mind are being used, what is perceived are not percepts tied to physical objects but rather images derived from sense data but elaborated differently. When we remember, especially if we have photographic memories, we are dealing with counterparts of percepts but experiencing them and manipulating them in another space and time. We are operating at a level of ourselves in which we can move images about freely and combine them in ways that would be impossible if they were direct percepts. This freedom in space is paralleled by a similar freedom in time. In memory we move back into the past; in planning we move forward into the future. As far as we know, we are the only species with this kind of freedom. This means that our bodies must be part of much larger communication systems than those of other animals, since we remain firmly embodied while moving through space and time in these various ways.

There is, however, another and more interesting way of seeing with the eyes of the mind. When recalling, planning, or even fantasizing, we are employing images that are already known. The first artist to draw a unicorn did not create something entirely new, but only combined familiar images in a new way. Imagination rearranged the phenomenal world without actually altering its contents—played with images horizontally, as it were. Really new insights, insights that add to the phenomenal world and extend its boundaries, come about when the eyes of the mind are trained on the transcendental, on what is still only potentially phenomenal. This involves a vertical focusing that may be quite unconscious but that is present whenever insight penetrates into areas where there are as yet no images, only the suspicion that there is something there to be discovered. Those who work on frontiers, whether of philosophy, art, or science, are probing after images that do not yet exist. They are at the interface between the phenomenal and the transcendental, between forms and the creative void out of which the known universe emerges.

This is where true morphogenesis takes place. Explorers in this region are trying to find they know not what and in the process generate new ways of seeing. They turn intuitions into images, which may become material objects or remain at mental levels as fructifying ideas that fire the imagination of others and lead to changes at the physical level only indirectly. Because creative geniuses can do this, the body must somehow be involved with the transcendental, though the boundary between what can be perceived and what cannot differs so widely among species. None, as far as we know, shares the human capacity to reach out to the transcendental, to encompass it and draw it into the phenomenal world. There must be special mechanisms that enable human beings to penetrate intuitively into the imageless void and bring down and give expression to insights—give them "a local habitation and a name." It can only be at the end of a process that a glimmer of an idea can become a well-reasoned article in a learned journal, a Pietà by Michelangelo, or a symphony by Mozart. At all stages of the process the body must cooperate as a mediating tool.

7
A Tantric Model:
Subtle Bodies, Chakras, and Kundalini

*N*o existing Western theory has yet been able to explain how the body and mind interact within the context of the personality as a whole. As a result we Westerners know a great deal more about our machines than about ourselves. Instead of being the originators of new ways of seeing, we are progressively degenerating into machine-minders, largely because we have allowed ourselves to contract in our own minds as a function of the way we confront the universe. We seem to ask too little of both it and ourselves.

Various phenomenological models already exist outside science as this is understood in the West. People in search of more holistic theories of human personality have been borrowing piecemeal from a number of them. One that investigates the inner constitution of man and the universe in some detail is Tantric Hinduism. This version of Hinduism differs from Vedanta, which is the form first popularized in the West. Nevertheless, I think Tantra may in the long run be found to be more useful as a scientific model. Both are phenomenologies, but whereas Vedanta regards the phenomenal world as purely the illusory product of the mind and the senses and tends to turn away from it, Tantra sees in it reality obscured by veils of matter. To know it may not be to know reality, but neither is knowledge about it a compounding of ignorance. Until the obscuring veils of matter drop away, truth and ultimate reality necessarily elude our comprehension, but partial knowledge is not illusory. It is phenomenal but useful in dealing with the world that we actually live in.

Tantra divides the cosmos into many levels and envisages human beings as selves encased in interpenetrating sheaths made up of the energies, or "stuff," of these many levels. This fits in well with the idea of sheaths as multiple bodies of communication in a unitary communications network. Tantric sages consistently speak of man as having not only several bodies but also *chakras* (force centers) and *nadis* (force channels), which enable energies to be conveyed from one body to another. While Western science has concentrated on the densest levels of this system and accumulated an enormous amount of data about them, Indian science has given priority to the subtler force fields. These must, I think, have been visible to the yogis who compiled the relevant treatises, for they write in a manner that suggests that they have actually seen what they describe. This is far from impossible. As we have seen, the research summarized by Dr. Karagulla shows that such extensions of awareness are more common even today than is generally realized. Several of Karagulla's subjects report seeing such centers and being able to use them diagnostically. Mrs. Bendit also noted their presence as focal points in the vital etheric field.

Tantricists analyze the complex of sheaths, or fields, that constitute the human being into three bodies and a transcendental self associated with them but not determined by them. The phenomenal part of the human person, or embodied self, consists of a subtle body, the vehicle for the expression of mind; the dense physical body, which is regarded as a passive "food sheath" controlled from above; and, connecting the two, a vitality body or "life vehicle." It is through this tripartite phenomenal personality that the transcendental self must be actualized if it is to find physical expression.

The personality, as a system of fields or bodies, forms around its transcendental core in a descending order, mind emanating from spirit, life from mind, and the dense body from all three working together on matter. Only after this process has reached the physical level can the personality gradually evolve into an instrument capable of manifesting the full range of powers that exist potentially in the transcendental, spiritual self. Seen from this point of view, evolution is the actualizing of this potential. What Western science calls evolution is only the physical component of a multilevel process. It is the story of the forms that these forces use as they work their way into matter, an account of the peopling of the earth with entities capable of responding to progressively finer forces. Humanity can only enter the picture, for instance, when physical structures have evolved that

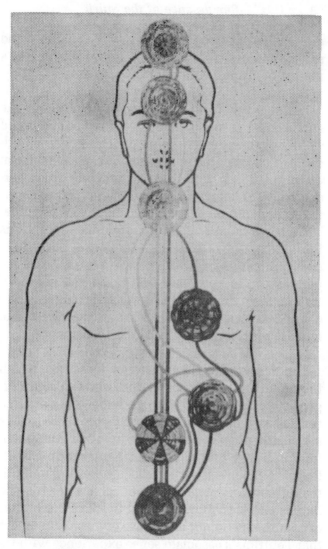

Fig. 1. Chakras and Nadis (from C. W. Leadbeater, The Chakras).

are capable of embodying not only life but mind and self-awareness. From then on evolution is less a matter of structure than of consciousness.

In the Hindu form of Tantric psychobiology the subtle body, or mental body, is said to be composed of four types of mental energy. The finest is *buddhi*, which gives the mind detachment so that it can distinguish self from other, perceiver from perceived. Next comes *ahangkara*, which gives I-ness to thought and makes self-consciousness possible. Then there is *manas*, which organizes sensations into perceptions. This is an important part of the communications network between the sensory apparatus of the body and the individual center of awareness in the self. Finally, there is *chitta*, which energizes memory and recall and therefore, like manas, plays an important role in perception.

Tantricists distinguish between the senses, which they place in the sensory mind, and the sense organs, which they place in the body. This distinction is based on the fact that, while the sense organs are clearly physical, sensation involves consciousness in a way that neural mechanisms do not. In terms of Arkle's theories, discussed in chapter 5, the former work at electrochemical levels while the latter operate in more ethereal fields of our bodies of communication. It is because of these differences that Tantricists associate sense experience with intangible structures and pathways, chakras and nadis, as well as with the sense organs. It is in these chakras (force centers) and nadis (force channels) that the energy exchanges take place that convert the impacts registered by the nerves into the patterns of mixed energies that underlie the perception of images.

According to Tantric theory sensations do not become perceptions as we know them until they undergo a rapid integrative process. First, they must be synthesized selectively by manas, assisted by chitta. They then have to be converted into aspects of our own personal experience by ahangkara, and finally they must be given meaning and relevance by the finest of the four mental energies, buddhi. Responses to the environment depend on how events are interpreted at the center of awareness at the end of this process. Here Arkle's distinction between matter-consciousness and matter-self-consciousness is germane. For instance, we cannot assume that animals are either self-aware or able to form relevant concepts. They are not able to use the consciousness fields of ahangkara and buddhi. Such percepts as they have must be in the nature of impressions put together by manas and chitta at the level of the instinctive, sensory mind.

In human beings what is made of sensory inputs varies according to the degree of objectivity of which the individual is capable. Less evolved minds react emotionally in terms of instinctual needs and drives, although they contain a measure of I-ness not enjoyed by animals. Perceptions here are comprised of manas and chitta with a dash of ahangkara. People who are strongly influenced by their conditioning use their rudimentary buddhi to interpret everything in terms of socially accepted stereotypes. Independence of thought and action can only be exercised by people with minds and nervous systems capable of handling the full range of mental energies and blending them smoothly into the electrochemical energies of the physical body. This theory of mind-body coordination avoids the necessity of putting the two into separate realities.

The importance of the perceptual role of chitta, the force underlying memory and habit formation, is stressed by Sri Aurobindo, the modern Tantric systematizer. He regarded it as having two modes: as a passive principle it acts like a subconscious memory store, receiving impacts impartially from the environment; as an active principle it is the agent of recall, providing material from the memory store when required. It forms bundles of habits, holding them together in memory and so giving continuity to personality through a sense of continuing identity. At the level of what Sri Aurobindo calls the "desire soul" it ensures that the needs of the instinctive nature are met. Within nature as a whole, chitta assists in preserving the identity of species as bundles of reactions held together by a primitive form of memory. Cell memory would be of this type, as would be the molecular memory that governs the specificity of chemical compounds. It ensures that each entity, from crystal to man, "remembers itself" and so goes on being itself, behaving in the future in a manner consistent with its past. It both underlies all continuities in nature and maintains the phenomenal world as a stable mental construct. As we have seen, it does the latter even for agnosia patients like Larry and John who remember in detail parts of things that they can no longer recognize as wholes. It is not chitta that fails them but buddhi, the mental energy that gives percepts meaning by categorizing them in terms of what they are.

Chitta is also necessary for shared perceptual worlds. In spite of the fact that different species concentrate on different aspects of the environment, there seems little doubt that all members of the same species form perceptual habits that they hold in common. It is possible to think of genes as encoded memory stores passed on from generation to generation, maintaining specificity as well as continuity of species over time. At a simpler level the memory store would be preserved by mitotic cell division, which ensures that each half develops into a daughter cell identical to its parent. If some phenomenon akin to memory is responsible for the specificity of fundamental particles and chemical elements, we arrive at Teilhard de Chardin's conception of matter and consciousness interlocked at every level and evolving together. It would also mean that there is no such thing as a purely physical entity or a purely physical universe. If this is so— and it looks as if it is—it confirms the need for a more integral as well as a more phenomenological approach to model building in both scientific and environmental studies. Our failure so far to achieve such an approach may explain why we get so many of our answers wrong when trying to improve the quality of life.

The energies of the life vehicle or vitality body the Tantricists call *prana*, from a word that means "life" or "breath." The life fields registered by Burr's voltmeter would presumably be prana fields. They would also be the major energies at work in

Mrs. Bendit's vital etheric field. The term "prana" is used in two different ways in Tantric treatises, and, if it is borrowed, the distinction between the two needs to be understood. In one usage there are pranas operating as bridging forces at all energy levels, linking the subtle and physical bodies. The other usage is employed by Sri Aurobindo to distinguish between life forces that unify mind and body on the one hand and forces that work in the body to maintain it as a living system on the other. He gave the name "psychic prana" to the first group and "physical prana" to the second.

This distinction is particularly useful when differentiating between the two parts of the auras seen by sensitives. They have a denser central section that follows the outline of the body, interpenetrating it and extending slightly beyond it. This is what is often called the "etheric double" because it is composed of etheric counterparts of the dense body and its component organs and tissues. It would have been into this part of the aura that Mrs. Bendit would look when working with her husband and his medical colleagues. Its close association with the health of the body means that the energies circulating in it would be physical rather than psychic pranas.

Beyond the etheric double is a roughly ovoid area in which forces move in a much less defined way. These auras usually appear as colors to clairvoyant vision so that, in order to analyze their interactions, one must first learn the sensitive's color language. This fact was drawn to my attention by a research officer of the College of Psychic Studies when I was considering a clairvoyant investigation into what my hands were doing in the healing situation. He suggested that employing a second sensitive as a control would only cause confusion. Each clairvoyant apparently develops his or her own symbolic and color language to interpret what is seen. These individual differences are presumably due to the fact that most sensitives develop their gifts in isolation. Those trained in groups are more likely to share a common language, which in turn would probably differ from that of other groups. The situation is much the same with people learning their various national and local idioms. Scientists who plan to use sensitives would need to be prepared to do a good ideal of interpreting themselves, as they had to do in the early days of electron microscopy and still have to do when breaking new ground.

It is in the etheric double that Sri Aurobindo's physical pranas are at work, while the more ethereal colored area reflects the movements of the finer psychic pranas. Some sensitives report seeing chakras on the surfaces of both the outer aura and the etheric double, while others place them only in the double.

When prana is withdrawn, organisms are said to die. This is because the life vehicle then disentangles itself from what Tantricists call the "chemical body," or "food sheath." This chemical body is the energy field of a set of forces belonging to the dense physical level of matter, the kundalini forces. What is meant by "kundalini" badly needs clarification not only if science is to make use of Tantric models but also because 'kundalini experiences' are being increasingly talked about. They

are being sought by some as life-enhancing and experienced by others as 'bad trips'. Kundalini yoga
has been widely misunderstood in the East as well
as in the West, as I discovered when researching
the kundalini concept for my book *Kundalini in the
Physical World*. As I have learned since my book
was published, kundalini is an anathema to many
seeking yogic enlightenment and a concept not
taken seriously even by scientists interested in
nature's finer forces. This is unfortunate, for the
more that I have researched in this area, the more
I have come to understand how the dense body and
its many associated bodies and fields may be interrelated. This understanding involves unseen forces
such as kundalini.

Both as a nurse and as a psychologist I have been
consistently challenged by the mind-body problem.
As a nurse I became quickly fascinated by physiology and the marvelous ways in which the body responds to all the demands we put upon it in health
and all the efforts it makes to correct imbalances
created by bad habits of diet and posture. Perhaps
most fascinating of all is the immune system, with
its capacity both to fight disease and to cleanse the
body of the detritus of such wars once won. When
I went on to study psychology and to carry my interest in health from that of bodies to that of persons, it never seriously occurred to me that body
and mind were not functionally interrelated. A part
of me has always assumed the sort of holistic psychobiology that I am advocating here. My problem
has always been to discover exactly how higher
energies affect the body and sensations become images in the mind. What is the physiology? What are
the mechanisms?

Theosophy has adopted and elaborated many ideas from the East, both speculatively and on the evidence of clairvoyant vision. Much has been written about the chakras and about prana but comparatively little about kundalini beyond the fact that both it and prana circulate in the chakras and in the body. Those writing about kundalini yoga primarily concentrate upon it as a force residing in a center or chakra, at the base of the spine, which in enlightened states rises through the chakras along the spine to the top of the head. Sri Aurobindo speaks of it as being able to move both up and down. There is little mention of it as an earth force found in all forms of dense matter. To discover this important fact, I had first to research the Tantric treatises translated from the Sanskrit by Sir John Woodroffe, the best known of which is *The Serpent Power*.

The familiar portrayal of the seven major chakras and the three largest nadis, arranged like a caduceus with the chakras (sometimes called "lotuses") spaced along the central rod, is an image derived from kundalini yoga. It is up the central nadi that kundalini is said to rise into the chakras on its journey upwards. Misguided enthusiasts from time to time meditate on these chakral centers and try by conscious effort to raise kundalini and so obtain enlightenment. Some of those who report "bad trips" have played this game. Its dangers have led serious spiritual directors to condemn this form of yoga, particularly in the West.

In another place I hope to write about my later researches into the relation of kundalini, the chakras, and the dense body in more detail. Here

I propose only to deal with the insights that I have gained from exploring the possible reasons why the Indian sages placed prana in the life vehicle and confined kundalini forces to the physical body which they called the chemical body. It was a long time before the importance of the word "chemical" struck me. Kundalini has been so extensively discussed in connection with unusual experiences that there is a tendency to think of it in terms of consciousness rather than of chemistry. For instance, the yogis link kundalini movements to changes in the chakras and associate the different chakras with various modes of conscious experience. Itzaak Bentov, who was interested in the underlying physiology of kundalini experiences, offered a theory of their bodily correlates. In his contribution to *Kundalini: Psychosis or Transcendence* he suggested that they were due to stresses caused by evolutionary developments of the nervous system. His theory was ingenious and useful, but it was based on resonances set up by pulsations in the body, producing electromagnetic fields. It was a theory about electronic and mechanical forces, not about chemical changes.

The answer to my problem came only after *Kundalini in the Physical World* was published and I had turned my attention from kundalini as a force present throughout physical nature to how it worked in the human body. As some readers may know, theosophical writers about the chakras have always associated each of the major chakras with one or other of the ductless glands. C. W. Leadbeater in his book *The Chakras* also made connections between them and various plexuses of the sympathetic nervous system. Most theosophical

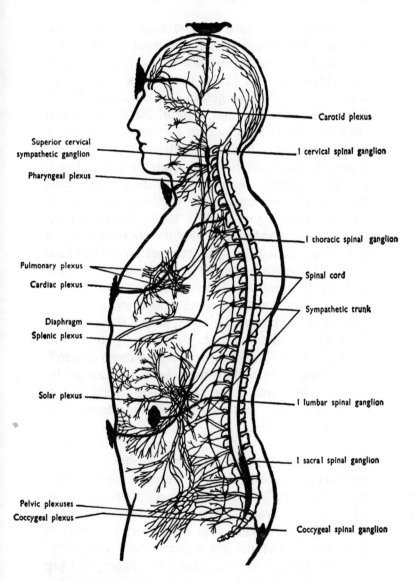

Fig. 2. The Chakras and the Nervous System (from C. W. Leadbeater, The Chakras).

writers, however, whether deriving their information from intuitive or from clairvoyant sources, have
stressed their endocrine rather than their neural as-
sociations. In view of the prevailing tendency in
science to relate changes in consciousness to the
behavior of the nervous system, the theosophical
emphasis on the endocrine system was an interesting deviation. It was a justifiable deviation and
a surprising one when one considers that Leadbeater's theories were put forward in 1927. Alice
Bailey's first reference to the matter in her *Treatise
on Cosmic Fire* goes back to 1923, though her definitive treatment of it in *Esoteric Healing* was not
published until 1953. The transaction of the Theosophical Research Center in England on the subject *Vital Magnetic Healing*, dates from 1935.
Though they are in general agreement about the
pairing of chakras and glands, not all these writers
were at one about which gland was paired with
which chakra. This is an area where more research
is needed. Where they have been vindicated by
scientific research is their emphasis on the importance of glands, not least in the importance they
gave to the pineal.

The seventeenth-century philosopher Descartes,
whose famous formula *Cogito ergo sum*—"I think,
therefore I am"—led to the development of scientific dualism, was the first to give a key role to the
pineal gland. Aware that his theories tended to
divide the individual into separate mental and bodily parts, he looked for a means of bridging the gap
and came up with the pineal, which he called the
seat of the soul. Because science dispensed with
the soul, Descartes, in spite of his efforts, fathered
the dichotomy of mind and body that has bedev-

Chakras and Glands (from Alice Bailey, Esoteric Healing, p. 202. Reprinted by permission of Lucis Publishing Co.).

iled philosophy ever since. It is even called "Cartesian dualism."

As technology developed, science and philosophy drew further apart and "speculative ideas" became increasingly suspect. This may account for the fact the endocrinologists neglected the pineal gland for so long. It was only in the 1960s that a few eminent scientists decided to make it a respectable object of study. The results surprised them, as was clearly shown in the papers of the participants at the first conference on the subject, held in Mexico City in 1970. It was there that it was christened "the regulator of regulators," a role that would not have come as a surprise to Descartes.

The history of endocrinology is a fascinating story of the search for the hormones that regulate bodily activity. Hormones are the messenger or facilitating molecules that switch cellular processes on and off and so determine how organs and tissues develop and what they do. In the 1920s when *The Chakras* was published, endocrinology was in its infancy. Research was concentrated on assigning their functions separately to the various ductless glands. The aim was to find out which hormones were secreted by which glands and what each governed. By the 1950s when *Esoteric Healing* was published, it had been discovered that the thyroid gland exerted a regulatory action on the rate at which the body burned up nutrients in order to fuel its various activities—its basal metabolic rate. It was obviously an important regulator. By the 1960s it was clear that the pituitary gland was a regulator of an even higher order. In conjunction with the nerve masses of the hypothalamus it exerted a controlling influence over so wide a range of activities involving other glands that it was thought that the master regulator had been found. It was only after research finally was directed to the pineal that this was disproved. It has become progressively clear that the pineal can override the powers of the hyperthalamo-pituitary complex. It does this by inhibiting their hormone-releasing mechanisms. It is primarily, though not exclusively, a switcher-off.

I found this last fact particularly interesting since it suggested a physical means whereby one's wider self could switch off the apparatus through which the conscious self controls one's actions and takes command itself. In order to do this, it would pre-sumably have to do two things. First, it would have to inhibit activities of the brain that subserve con-sciousness. It would have to do this selectively, however. For instance, in the healing clinic, though less in the examination hall, I was fully perceptually aware. What I no longer consciously controlled was what I did. Second, it would have to take over the direction of the motor nervous system so that the body acted efficiently and appropriately. Between the powers of the hypothalamo-pituitary complex to release and those of the pineal to inhibit selec-tively it now seems feasible to presume that it can do both these things.

What is surprising is that the pineal exercises its controlling influence despite the fact that it has practically no connection with the cerebral nerve centers that surround it. It passes its chemical mes-sengers into the blood and the cerebrospinal fluid in the third ventricle at the center of the brain, in-to which it projects. It influences the nervous sys-tem indirectly through a widespread network of cells that, like itself, are both glands and linked functionally with the nervous system, the APUD (amine precursor uptake decarboxytator) cells of the nervous-endocrine system. APUD cells are neuro-transmitters because their hormones are chemical substances that enable nerve impulses to be trans-mitted from one nerve fiber to another. Here at last was the bridging system that I had been looking for, a chemical organization that linked the chakras and major ductless glands on the one hand and the brain and major divisions of the nervous system on the other. It is, moreover, a system capable of mediating an enormous range of energy exchanges. From the standpoint of a holistic psychobiology its discovery was an event of great significance.

The diffuse nervous-endocrine system is a net-work of cells scattered throughout the body. Each APUD cell is a minute chemical factory. The chem-ical messengers, or hormones, that they manufac-ture are neurotransmitters such as dopamine, the transmitter that is defective in Parkinson's disease. The extensive APUD network secretes and stores a wide range of these messenger substances, in-cluding adrenalin and noradrenalin, so vital for the body's flight or fight responses, once thought to be found in the adrenal glands above the kidneys. In the 1980 edition of *Gray's Anatomy* forty varieties of APUD cells were already listed, all with different functions, and more are still being discovered. Each cell is capable of secreting its own specific hormone directly into the blood wherever it is needed and so speeding up the work of the major ductless glands, each of which is strictly localized.

As neurotransmitters the APUD cells really deter-mine how nerves behave and therefore what kinds of nerves they are. In other words, chemical forces are responsible for the content of the messages that the electronic forces convey along the nerves to the brain or by reflex action to organs and tissues. If chemical forces are kundalini forces and electronic forces are pranic, this is compatible with two statements made by Tantricists about kundalini: that kundalini is the ruling power in the world of dense matter and that kundalini and prana circulate together through the body. Nowhere can this be more true than in this system of cells that are both nerves and glands, chemical factories and sources of electrical impulses.

As part of the glandular system APUD cells fall within kundalini's chemical organization, working through the blood and cerebrospinal fluid and utilizing the kidneys and lymphatic system to control chemical thresholds and maintain a normal water balance in tissues and organs. As part of the nervous system they influence the way prana flows in the autonomic and central nerve pathways. Clusters of APUD cells may also be found to be associated with acupuncture points. The meridians of acupuncture, which I have never been able to link with the nervous system in any direct way, may be energy pathways for a different but supplementary pranic energy. The range of life forces in the prana sheath need not coincide with that of the electromagnetic spectrum.

Prana, kundalini, and their respective "realms" can perhaps be best differentiated by considering how bodies disintegrate when prana is said to be withdrawn at death. It is the chemical constituents that are left to join the general pool of molecules available for recycling and use in other dense bodies of one sort or another. The question of whether life fields continue to surround a discarnate self or whether the life vehicle also disintegrates into a mass of energy particles is an interesting one but not relevant here. What is germane is that the disintegration of a living organism into a mere collection of chemicals tells us two things about bodies: that there is some integrative element that structures them into the living forms that we know and that there must exist forces that provide the chemical building blocks without which bodies would lack the solidity of material objects. It is these latter forces that are responsible for what we can see with ordinary vision. Without them objects as we know them would disappear, as fundamental particles appear to do, into another dimension. It is because kundalini forces give phenomenal existence to solid objects that Tantricists call Kundalini Shakti *Shabdabrahman in bodies,* the creator of bodies, and the Earth is her realm.

One final point should be made before I leave the Tantric model. It is important not to be put off by the oriental proclivity for writing symbolically and deifying natural forces. Kundalini and prana are forces in the same sense that gravity and electricity are forces. Moreover, they must be understood to be unknowable in themselves just as gravity and electricity are unknowable in that they can neither be seen nor experienced directly. We infer them and contrive devices that enable us to use them, but they themselves remain elusive. Gravity and electricity may, however, be forces of different orders. It may be because physicists do not distinguish between them that they fail to unify their fields of forces. It may be that gravity is a kundalini force, different in kind from the forces of the electromagnetic spectrum. It might be a good idea to distinguish more clearly between the "realms" of chemistry and physics. This might help us to clarify the limits of adaptation of organisms both in respect of our own food sheaths and in respect of the chemical bodies of plants and animals. Above all, it might serve to keep within bounds our Promethean efforts to harness energy in ways that the chemical organization of the Earth cannot assimilate. Pollution and the proliferation of allergies and increasingly resistant bacteria already warn us that, in our experiments with genetic materials and artificial substances, we may be straining nature's powers of adjustment beyond its safety limits.

8
The Body and Its Selves

*I*t is striking to notice how often, especially in the work of endocrinologists, embryologists, and cytologists (who research cell structure), one comes across the comment, "The mechanism involved is still obscure." In biology, as in physics, exploring entities from the material side seems progressively to bring to light finer and finer structures until, finally, they can be traced no further. They seem to disappear into another dimension, to be operating still but in a different though related space. The oriental view that matter is spiritual energy precipitated down through mental and vital levels into dense physical forms is quite compatible with the idea of physical mechanisms associated with those of a higher order as part of a single system. In this case, of course, many mechanisms underlying bodily activity would naturally appear obscure until such time as they could be studied at their higher levels.

The possibility that physical structures may be dependent on energy sources outside those currently recognized by science does not readily occur to the modern Western mind. This is in part due to our need to see in order to believe. At every stage unusual phenomena have to prove their reality, preferably in the laboratory. Even then, those who have not actually seen for themselves remain only half-convinced and are easily persuaded to doubt the evidence. Another source of resistance to the idea of finer forces is the fear that their discovery may have dangerous consequences. With every new force comes the intellectual urge to understand it, followed by the Promethean urge to harness it. It is mainly at the harnessing stage that resistance arises. At first people refused to eat food cooked on gas stoves for fear of carbon-monoxide poisoning. At first simple electrical appliances aroused fears hardly comprehensible today. We are in the midst of the same reaction to nuclear power, which of course can have disastrous effects until we learn how to use it safely.

Many forces are dangerous if mishandled; it is just that unfamiliar ones arouse the added fear of the unknown. It is not the resources of the universe that we should fear, however, but scientific hubris and our tendency to assume that these forces are easier to manage than they actually are. We are using nuclear power before we have learned how to produce it without simultaneously producing a long-lasting, pervasive, and highly toxic type of waste. A little learning is indeed a dangerous thing, especially when greedy promoters are pressing for quick results or research funds are limited. But our worst enemies are those that the scientists of the first Renaissance avoided, insufficient respect for nature and a tendency to oversimplify it because its complexity is so subtle. We are still making new discoveries about electromagnetism, for instance. There may even be electromagnetic forces as yet unknown to us. From what has been said about APUD cells there is clearly much about the chemical forces at work in nature that is yet to be uncovered.

It is because most of its investigation into forces is going on in a materialistic setting that hubris in science is so dangerous. It is also a major cause of the frustration of spirit that I spoke of earlier. Ordinary people know instinctively that they are being treated as some sort of superior animal and resent it. They know that they are more than that, and it is not surprising that their resentment is often shown in inconvenient and socially unacceptable ways. Their protests are unlikely to stop until they are offered a philosophy of life and a view of themselves that expands them and satisfies their sense of human dignity at the same time. This is why the solution of the mind-body problem is so vital. We need to see ourselves not as superanimals in a world of objects but as human beings in a world of many levels rich in possibilities for growth and creativity.

This is also why the discovery of the diffuse nervous-endocrine system is so important and why its holistic implications should be followed up. It needs to be studied in a context of human beings as multiple field systems operating on many levels. It is only then that we can begin to think of the body in relation to other aspects of the total self and not merely in terms of physiology and anatomy conceived materialistically. For instance, we can then note that all the complex activities of the endocrine glands and the diffuse nervous-endocrine system take place below the threshold of consciousness. It must be into this subconscious vegetative organization that physical prana is fed to keep the body going—and without troubling our conscious selves at all. There are also links between the autonomic and central nervous systems that enable the body to carry out a great deal of motor activity in a purely reflexive way. This is also the level of subconscious perception. Using the Tantric model, one could say that in these activities manas patterns sensory inputs and chitta contributes elements from the memory stores, while psychic prana is used to channel their combined energies into the physical body. This enables us to carry out many tasks quite effectively without having to think about them.

It is because of all this very efficient subconscious activity that the conscious self has so much freedom to act without having to tell the nerves and tissues what to do at every point. It also makes it possible for other aspects of the personality to use the body without the conscious self necessarily participating or even being consulted. In cases where there are pathological splits in the personality, various subpersonalities can take command without the conscious self knowing what they are doing. In mediumship there is a voluntary standing aside of the conscious self to make way either for some other segment of the medium's own personality or for what claims to be a discarnate entity borrowing the medium's body for the purpose of communication. It was presumably the body's subconscious systems as well as its organs that my more knowledgeable self took over both in the examination hall and in the healing clinic. It is no doubt because of its ready availability for use by different aspects of the total self that Tantricists view the dense body as a passive principle, the outer instrument of the self, the mind in the subtle body being the inner instrument.

Whether we call the various aspects of the total self subpersonalities or think of them as lesser selves, it is important to remember that they all have common access to the machinery of the body. It is the body that gives us our sense of continuing identity. It also enables us to feel that we are a single coherent whole, however inconsistently we behave from time to time. We are not just selves, as we tend to think of ourselves; nor are we just bodies, as scientists tend to regard us; we are embodied selves. Our bodies give us our sense of unity in time and space; our selves give us infinite possibilities for self-expression and role-taking. Both give human personality its richness and scope for development. The body anchors us in the physical world, while at subtler levels the self can enhance its potentialities by trying out different attitudes and new ways of perceiving and behaving.

In this the conscious self plays a directing role. Its job is to decide on ends, relying on the subconscious levels of the self and on the body to provide the means by which the ends are achieved. This is the level at which integration of the personality can occur. We are far from being integrated or even consistent. We can all vouch for this from our own experience. We can be confident and outgoing with our friends and self-doubting and hesitant when intellectual superiors patronize us. We can be genial colleagues at work and grumbling and critical at home. Most of us are full of contradictions. Frequently we fail to achieve our ends through clumsiness or bad judgment. This is often because the body is getting two sets of messages: the conscious self is saying, "Let us do this"; but at the same time some self-doubting lesser self is saying, "We can't manage it." The result is inevitably an unsuccessful effort or, at best, a performance below the level of our real potential. The body cannot simultaneously serve two masters, which is why integration of the various sides of ourselves into a consistent whole is so desirable.

The question now arises: what is the self that is so much wiser than the conscious self that I met so unexpectedly during my philosophy examination, and how does one learn to relate to it? There is no evidence to suggest that the entities or subpersonalities that take over the body in mediumship are necessarily of a superior intellectual or spiritual order. They may be, but I have heard mediums speak in trance at levels well below those of their own conscious utterances. Such people often have a loose personality structure and an inferiority complex so that one suspects that some aspect of themselves is trying to imbue them with more confidence through the interest their mediumship arouses in others. On the other hand, it may be unconsciously contrived to express a side of the personality not given scope in real life.

I recall an interesting case of a very intelligent woman who fell into the latter category. She had a degree in economics and a job in business. In

search of wider interests she had joined a development circle at a psychic center. In the course of her
training two guides had emerged, Madame Curie
and a nun. The nun particularly surprised her, as
she had long considered herself a materialist. The
presence of Madame Curie was equally surprising
but most flattering. She came to me because she was
in doubt about taking up mediumship professionally. What was uncovered in the course of our talks
together were two most suggestive facts. One was
that at some point she had wanted to be a doctor,
and the other that she had gone through a very
religious phase in her teens. After a while she came
spontaneously to the conclusion that it was highly
unlikely that she had the actual Madame Curie "on
tap," as it were. It seemed much more likely that
a frustrated doctor in herself was dramatizing itself
in order to get a hearing and that Madame Curie
was the model she sought to copy. The nun was
a more general symbol of the spiritual side of her
nature, which she had suppressed but clearly never
completely subdued.

Apart from the "selves" corresponding to the
various subpersonalities that constitute our psychological makeup, based largely on our different real-
life roles, there are two major selves in all of us.
One of these is our familiar conditioned personal
self and the other an elusive transcendental self, of
which some of us become aware and about which
all religions speak in one way or another. In Hinduism this is clearly recognized as the divine self
within, the Brahman self. Christianity is more am-
bivalent. Sometimes it speaks of the Christ within,
but there is also a tendency to put God and Christ

outside the self and see the human being as only a possible vessel or channel of divine grace. Buddhism speaks of our Buddha nature, which is ourselves in our true being as distinct from our conditioned being.

Sri Aurobindo, to whose Tantric writings I have already referred, makes a distinction along the same lines that fits in well with an evolutionary view of personality. He speaks of a superficial self and a subliminal self. The superficial self is the conditioned one with which we tend to identify; the subliminal self represents our true nature, towards which we are evolving and which must ultimately break through the limitations of our conditioning and take over the direction of our lives. In the East this psychological process would be understood to occur within a context of reincarnation and karma in order to allow the individual to mature over many lifetimes and be given opportunities to correct mistakes. Karma is sometimes called the law of cause and effect. It can be good or bad. Its aim is corrective. If we cause suffering, we must experience suffering in order to learn to live in harmony with others and serenely with ourselves.

The subliminal self is so called because, in the course of our development as persons, it remains for the most part unsuspected, below the threshold of our conscious awareness. Its action is like that of the Aristotelean *entelechy*, the mysterious element within that ensures that everything fulfills its own nature and does not develop into something else. Just as the acorn cannot grow into anything but an oak tree, so the subliminal self is that within each one of us that matures in conformity with our own uniqueness. In the course of reincarnation it surfaces until, in a final state of enlightened spirituality, it ousts the superficial self with which we have for so long identified. It is only then that our divine and human natures can function together as one.

In any one lifetime the subliminal self experiences the phenomenal world through a particular set of sheaths and a physical body of a particular sex. This constitutes the superficial self, the this-life personality. It can also be thought of as the subliminal self adjusted by karma to meet the challenges and learn the lessons presented by the environment into which it has been born.

Superficial selves are the combined products of our genetic and social conditioning and our acquired judgments about ourselves and the world. The coexistence of this conditioned self and the subliminal self operating below the threshold of consciousness sets up in us a creative tension between the self with which we identify and the unrecognized one struggling to express itself through us. It is this tension that fuels spiritual growth through the friction it causes and the urge to overcome the discomfort it generates.

For Freud all our conflicts are within our personal selves. His superego was merely conscience as a product of our moral indoctrination in childhood. Its role was primarily to keep in check the primitive, genetically based id, which would otherwise seek its own selfish satisfactions without let or hindrance. As a result of the continual struggle between id and superego the hard-pressed conscious self, the ego, developed a tendency to push its problem children into a part of the psyche Freud called the unconscious ego and Jung the personal unconscious.

Jung's own inner experience forced him to recognize a higher organization within him, which was not the result of his childhood conditioning. It could not be reduced to the superego but rather opposed, often uncomfortably, the religious and moral assumptions of his parents. It could be said that from an early age Jung was aware of a subliminal self. He came to think of it as a final cause in the Aristotelean sense, a not yet known force, a not yet achieved Self, working constantly from within towards health and wholeness. Underlying the conflict between the conscious ego and its rejected "shadow" in the personal unconscious there was for Jung a sort of tug-of-war going on between the conscious personal ego and a transcendental Self akin to Sri Aurobindo's subliminal self. The reduction of these two sets of conflicts he called the individuation process, which culminated with the Self making itself known in consciousness.

For Sri Aurobindo there was only one real conflict, that between the embodied self as it is as the result of karma, the conditioned superficial self, and the embodied self as it can be once the distortions produced by karmic necessity have been corrected, the subliminal self or personality in its divinely intended form. As a Tantric Hindu Sri Aurobindo does not leave the body out of this individuation process as religious and even Jungian psychologists tend to do. Hence, his integral yoga aims to achieve wholeness not only by reordering the psyche but by living in such a way that the personality is transformed into a fit instrument of the true self, body as well as soul.

Only those who have had some intimation of a transcendental presence in their own experience readily believe in it. We tend to divide into Freudians and Jungians on this issue. Many, however, are aware of tension between two sides of themselves that is not neurotic. According to Sri Aurobindo it arises when the subliminal self representing one's undistorted being is beginning to demand attention. One becomes increasingly aware of making spontaneous responses to situations as unwilled as they are apposite and effective. Sometimes these experiences are not recognized for what they are and are easily overlooked or forgotten. At other times they are so striking as to act as catalysts and alter one's entire life. It is experiences of this kind that force one to acknowledge the existence of an organization at work within that is of a higher order than that of the self with which we normally identify.

9

Healing and the Chakras

*M*y own belief in a subliminal self arose out of
the experiences I have already described, but what
intrigued me in subsequent years was how the intelligence that guided my hands controlled my
body. At a particularly bad time, when the treatment I was having for my back left me too tired to
see more than an occasional patient, it occurred to
me that I could perhaps find out. If I could heal
merely by putting myself in readiness, could I not
address myself to this knowledgeable entity and,
with crayons and paper before me, ask for an answer
to this question? The experiment seemed worth trying and, at worst, I could regard the exercise as oc-
cupational therapy.

In planning this I decided against automatic or
directed writing. I was too facile with words and
might influence the outcome without meaning to.
I therefore set out to contrive a question that could
be answered diagramatically. It had to be sufficiently clear-cut for the diagram to be simple and un-
ambiguous. From the outset I felt that I was
addressing some wiser part of myself and not a

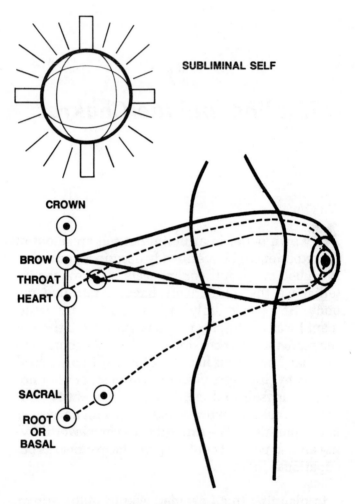

SUBLIMINAL SELF

CROWN

BROW

THROAT

HEART

SACRAL

ROOT
OR
BASAL

Fig. 3. Self-healing of a Back Injury.
The circles on the left represent the chakras, which are
actually along the spinal column. The circle on the right
represents the solar plexus chakra. Lines indicate the
flow of energy in the process of healing.

separate entity. Later I came to recognize it as my subliminal self. "How do you control the healing process?" I asked it.

Surprisingly, the answer came first into my mind very quietly in words: "By resonance." This in itself was interesting, for I had expected a drawing showing energy flowing from the subliminal self directly toward the body. This was apparently not the case. It worked by remote control so that there had to be an energy gap to be jumped at some point. This led me to ask more questions, which this time were answered diagramatically. In order to make my request as concrete as possible, I asked that I be shown a healing process directed at my back. In answer to this came the outline of a body in profile from neck to thigh. This was placed on the right of the page; there was nothing else. Then I asked, "Can I have a symbol for you?" This duly came, this time at the top of the page on the extreme left. It took the form of a cross in a circle surrounded by gold radiations. There was then another pause. Asking seemed important, so I said, "What about the process?"

The process should not have surprised me. Using different colors, a set of discs appeared directly under the symbol representing the subliminal self. They came in a descending order and were filled in by both clockwise and counterclockwise movements similar to the ones I used over the chakras in healing. Another set of discs was then drawn to the right of the first. I was given the impression of energy descending by stages, each stage involving some but not all the seven major chakras.

The first two sets of discs were parallel to the axis of the body and to the left of it. Only at the third stage was a disc placed to the right of the body in front of the solar-plexus area. Each line of rotating discs appeared to represent a subtler level of energy in the chakras than the one succeeding it, the one at the solar plexus operating closest to the chemical body. This impression was strengthened when colored lines were drawn linking the first two sets of chakras to the one in front of the body. Three colors were used to suggest the circulation of three types of energy, converging on the solar-plexus force center from which its energies were presumably dispersed via the etheric double to the appropriate target areas. Moreover, the way in which the linkages were made indicated an energy flow from above downward, since each colored line started under the subliminal-self symbol and ended at the body.

Though energy was shown passing through the chakras as one continuous circulation through three levels, at no point was there any direct connection between the symbol above and the movements depicted below. In this way my questions were answered, both confirming a gap and enlarging on the process controlled from above by the subliminal healer. I did many such drawings about patients later, from which I gathered that the process differed from patient to patient. It also became clear from the way I worked that their psychological condition influenced the state of the body so that no two healing sessions were ever the same. This was because what happened to the patient as a person between one visit and the next would necessarily have altered in many subtle ways the play of forces in the personality field as a whole.

When I asked my first question I emphasized that it was a general one. Relating it to my own back was intended merely to make it more concrete and easier to answer diagramatically. The answering drawing reflected this, for certain features proved common to all similar drawings done for patients. All started with a body and the subliminal-self symbol; all involved chakras; and in all cases the energy flow was from left to right or from above downwards. What differed was the order in which the chakras were activated and the nature of the force flowing through them. When working with others, the energy transmitted seemed to be a generalized healing force. In the diagram about my own body the self-healing process involved three specific energies, each represented by a different color and converging on the body by different routes. I assumed from this that, whereas three different levels of energy could be manipulated separately and directly by my own subliminal self, it apparently did not perform the same service for my patients. In their case a generalized force was fed into their personality fields and then differentiated by their own subliminal selves. This seemed to me much more satisfactory and lessened my fears that my hands might be making misguided intrusions into their energy fields. Provided that both their subliminal selves and mine were in charge, it seemed unlikely that much could go seriously wrong. This may not be the case in all healing, of course, but in my own work I increasingly came to feel that at every healing session—whether it involved hand healing,

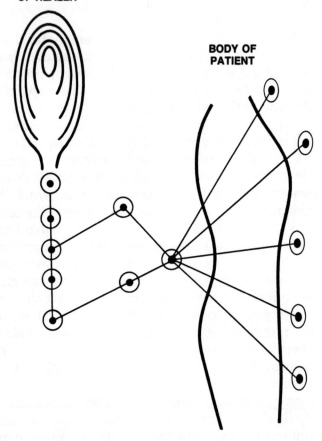

SUBLIMINAL SELF OF HEALER

BODY OF PATIENT

Fig. 4. Energy Flow during Healing.

The circles on the left represent the healer's chakras, with her subliminal self represented by the flame-like shape above. The circles on the right represent the patient's chakras. Lines indicate the energy flow during treatment.

counseling, or the discussion of paintings—two subliminal selves, mine and the patient's, were working in close cooperation.

The threefold arrangement in which the chakras were consistently represented in my diagrams suggested that one must regard them as mediating three distinct energies relating to different levels of our extended energy spectrum. This view is shared by numerous occult writers, but they usually speak as if the chakras existed in three separate bodies or sheaths and not, as I have come to believe, only in the life vehicle. In *Theories of the Chakras* Dr. Hiroshi Motoyama and Swami Satyananda write of chakras in the astral and causal bodies. Like Leadbeater in *The Chakras*, Motoyama also postulates a set of etheric centers. Swami Satyananda's third-level chakras seem to differ, for he most unusually places them in the dense physical body, in the brain, the nervous system, and the acupuncture points.

The disjunction between the symbol representing the subliminal self and the chakral field in my diagram, taken together with the statement that the subliminal self controls the healing process by resonance, seems to imply that the subliminal self in the subtle body manipulates the kundalini and pranic forces by remote control, using its "inner instrument" to bring about changes in its "outer instrument." This suggests affinities between consciousness fields and the pranic fields of the life vehicle that facilitate the transposition of mental into physical energy and vice versa. One gathers from the consistency of my diagrams that these energy exchanges are effected in the chakras and occur in stages, at least in certain healing situations and possibly as a general rule.

Returning to my original diagram with these ideas in mind, I saw that one could relate my first two sets of chakras to energies coming from the subtle body without necessarily placing them in it. They could represent different energy levels within the life vehicle mediating two types of psychic prana, one related to the rational and the other to the instinctive and emotional aspects of mind. In ill-health or anxiety states these may not be flowing through the chakras together as smoothly as they should. This could cause perturbations at the interfaces between levels, which would be experienced subjectively as psychological stress. The third set of chakras would presumably be concerned with physical prana, and it would be at this level that perturbations would begin to have physiological repercussions. It would thus be necessary to correct aberrations at all three chakral levels if the healing process were to produce a state of the life vehicle conducive to general wellbeing. What is ideally aimed at in healing of this sort is to put the patient as a person in touch with his or her own essential self and not merely to cure symptoms. Only by this means can wellbeing become a permanent state maintained from within. This is what the best practitioners of holistic medicine are already trying to do.

In subsequent paintings done for information about the interrelations between different aspects of the personality I seldom found myself interpreting in terms of bodies. Images seemed to be used to distinguish between selves, each of which had access to the body and all of which were, in a variety of ways, connected with it, with one another, and with the subliminal self. This basic self, though it seemed to be aware of all that was going on throughout the personality, only interfered under certain conditions. It was here that the role of the conscious ego emerged as crucial. Its attitude can either activate or depotentiate the subliminal self. This is where free will comes in.

If we believe that wiser counsels can reach the conscious self from a teacher and healer within, this of itself seems to operate as an activator, and wisdom and power that would otherwise have remained transcendental and unavailable can flow down into phenomenal levels for our conscious use. This is perhaps why the New Testament places so much emphasis on faith. It seems to be necessary, if we wish to incarnate our full potential, that we believe such a consummation at least to be possible. Similarly, the desire to be made whole can be an implicit plea. We may not even be aware that our very attitude is an unconscious prayer. The converse is also true. If the conscious self refuses to accept that such an incarnation is possible, it is not. The subliminal self in such cases remains transcendental, unable to use the body or manifest its presence in our ordinary, everyday lives.

There is an intermediate state of mind, which lies between the outright rejection of the idea of a suprahuman or divine self and the explicit effort to incarnate it. It is very common among those interested in yoga. It is a state of mind in which the conscious self believes in the existence of the Guru or Lord within but feels that it is up to it to direct the process by means of which it is found and experienced. If the individual does not know how to go about finding it, he or she sets out to find a teacher in the world outside who does. People who act in this way can be lucky or unlucky. Their attitude may embody the implicit plea of which I have just spoken. This may enable them to be guided by their subliminal selves to those who can truly help. Or they may be poorly motivated and fall into all sorts of spiritual difficulties, some even causing severe physical or mental distress.

It is important to recognize that in order to become embodied, the self has to take on a specifically male or female body. I discovered this in the course of studying paintings done by myself and others. I found that the subliminal self was insistent that "the proper form" of men must be masculine and of women feminine. I was rather surprised by this, as I had entered into this work with Jungian expectations about the relation of the ego to the unconscious. In Jungian psychology there is a male-female complementarity with the anima as a feminine principle in the unconscious partnering the masculine conscious ego in men, and the animus as a masculine principle partnering the feminine conscious ego in women. These principles are seen as intermediaries between the ego and the Self in the individual's search for wholeness. The subliminal self in our work did not seem to need these intermediaries, the complementarity being between the subliminal self and the body. On the only occasion when I formulated a request for myself with the animus in mind, I produced such a bisexual monstrosity that I realized that I had gone wrong somewhere. Subsequent paintings made it clear that it was best to concentrate on defining problems and let the subliminal self select the images through which they were solved. Moreover, I found myself presented with images relating to problem-ridden parts of myself, often children or young adults, rather than to archetypes or archetypal situations. The one exception was the mandala. This was perhaps Jung's most favored image of the Self. It also seems to be a universal symbol of the wholeness of things, whether it be the universe or a human being.

The emphasis on sex in paintings may have been due to my explicit involvement of the body in framing my original questions. However, it also makes sense if the subliminal self is a segment of the true self trying to find its way into the phenomenal world in a particular lifetime. The sex of its body of manifestation must be highly relevant in defining the conditions with which it will have to contend—its karma, as the Hindus would say. The way in which the superficial self is modified by social factors is very different for men and women so that any whole-making process would necessitate correcting false self-evaluations caused by the sexual mores of particular societies. These presently operate greatly to the disadvantage of women, many of whom are sadly deformed and stunted by their low opinion of themselves, which their experience of life tends to reinforce. It is perhaps not sufficiently realized by many how hard it is for women to make their proper contribution to society. Not only do they have to fight an ethos that relegates them to unpaid domestic roles and then makes pay a measure of status; they have to fight the lack of self-confidence that has been bred into them by social attitudes that persistently devalue their potentialities in almost any type of work to which they are drawn outside the home. Not only do their thinking selves have to be freed from the results of this conditioning; their feeling selves have to be healed of their hurts.

It is important to remember that not only the subliminal and conscious selves have access to the body: so do all the subpersonalities that make up the superficial self and contribute to the inconsistencies and contradictions of human nature. This is why we can be pulled in so many directions and why our behavior is often so hard to control. Nevertheless, for much of our development this divided superficial self is paramount. It gets between us and our true selves. It depotentiates the subliminal self by denying it access to the physical body and therefore prevents it from helping us as much as it might in our daily lives. Fortunately, there seems to be one depotentiating power it does not have. It cannot destroy an inherent partnership that seems to exist between the subliminal self and the body. It is probably this partnership that enables the subliminal self to influence the body and the chakras of the life vehicle "by resonance." It must also be what enables it to bypass ego-controlled systems on appropriate occasions. Growth in wholeness would appear to be a two-pronged attack on distorting factors; from the subliminal self above and from the body and life vehicle below.

The body may be a passive principle in the sense that it can be controlled from above and from without. At the same time it sets the limits within which vital and mental forces must work in dense matter. These limits are defined by the ways in which chemical structures can behave in integrated systems and by the laws governing the extent to which they can be altered in growth or by disease or misuse. This is why kundalini forces are said to be paramount in the physical world. They are the determinants of form, including the forms through which life and mind gain physical expression. This is also why chakras are important energy transducers. Indeed, they may have developed integrally with the organs into which the energies they mediate must flow if the body is to be a living organism and a person a thinking being.

In a comparative study of subsequent paintings by myself and others I was given some idea how the actualization of spiritual potential comes about. As all Tantric yogis insist, it does indeed involve living in such a way that nothing impedes the passage of higher energies through the chakras. Once the distortions making for inconsistencies and divisions in the superficial self are removed, it appears that all types of forces can move so integrally through them that local disturbances at the various levels no longer occur. In psychological terms this means that the conscious, thinking mind and the instinctive, feeling mind work as one in carrying the intentions of true self into the body and so out into the field of action in the phenomenal world. From the manner in which the later paintings came I got the impression that it is not the chakras that we should work on but the distortions caused by conditioning.

There is nothing that I have discovered since which runs counter to this. I find myself in complete agreement with Sri Aurobindo. As the quality of one's life improves, as the subliminal self gains control, changes in the chakras take place automatically to allow consciousness to deepen and widen. This is because the whole-making process brings them into full activity and perfect alignment. Kundalini yoga is sometimes called *laya* yoga. "Laya" means dissolution. Many tend to think that this means the destruction of the ego, but closer examination suggests that the dissolution is not so much of the ego as of the impediments that have prevented it from seeing truly and so acting rightly.

As a postscript to this account of a teaching dialogue between my conscious and subliminal selves I should perhaps point out that I have no reason to suppose that the colors used to differentiate between the chakras represent their actual colors. I referred earlier to the fact that sensitives have their individual languages of color and symbol. My colors were given to me, and I found that they were used consistently within my own work. Others might well have the same information imparted in quite a different way. It has been noted by psychologists using painting therapeutically that they do not all give the same meaning to the same colors.

It would seem that the important thing is for therapist and patient to understand each other. They must speak the same language. It is immaterial what that language is.

An interesting instance of this came my way during my training analysis. My analyst, an eclectic with Jungian leanings, had acquired a patient who had previously been attending a Freudian psychiatrist. One day, bringing her his latest dream, he remarked that his dreams seemed to have changed completely since coming to her. Her comment to me was, "Of course. In analysis dreams are communications between the healer within the patient and the healer without. How could I help if his dreams did not come in a language I could interpret?"

I am sure people are quite right in thinking that much dreaming is more or less random. The brain may arrange new images in its memory banks while the mind is off-duty. But as soon as a communication situation is set up, they can become highly meaningful. I learned that in my own analysis. Those who have gone to sleep with problems and have dreamed the answers know it. Jung called dreams "the royal road to the unconscious." They enable us to contact sources of information in ourselves not readily available to our waking minds. The trouble is that our conscious minds use a different language and cannot easily understand that of imagery and symbol.

10
Religious Psychology and the Body

*T*he strong affinity between the body and the sub-liminal self was first brought home to me by the way the two cooperated when my conscious self was put out of action in the examination hall. There, brain, eye, and hand worked in perfect harmony with it. The ego was present, as indeed it must be where there is awareness of an experience as one's own, but it was there merely as the observer of an activity, set in motion by the conscious self, it is true, but no longer controlled by it.

That the partnership between the body and the subliminal self may be more effective when interference by the conscious self is minimal was implied by my behavior at the healing center. What was interesting there was the fact that it was not my conscious self that decided to stand aside. It was quietly bypassed though its intention—to be willing to heal and to learn why it had been told that it could—was honored meticulously. The experience also showed that the center of awareness, the ego or observer in us, can move from conscious self as agent to watch another self in action. This was a highly competent self in my case, but one that my limited conditioned self was not yet big enough to encompass.

I think that this may be how our individual sub-liminal selves gradually emerge. We become more aware of an agent at work within to which our bodies respond but with which we cannot yet com-pletely identify. We cannot deny that its actions are in some sense our own, since our bodies perform them, yet we do not feel that we can claim credit since we did not consciously direct the process that led up to them. In my case the capacity for a higher than normal quality of performance preceded the awarenss of an expanded conscious self. In others there seems to be perception of a subliminal self as a presence before actions from its level can arise spontaneously. There may be an introvert-extrovert temperamental basis for this difference, or it may depend on the degree to which the individual in-corporates the body into his image of the spiritual self.

There is a point of some importance to be made here. The subliminal self can be mistaken for a visiting presence, an angel, some great guru, even God. This is because, having been so long beyond our experience, it enters our ordinary consciousness first of all as a stranger. Another reason why its rela-tion to ourselves is difficult to recognize is that we can be aware of it before we can consciously iden-tify with it. That this was so in my case is clear from my reaction to its manifestation in the examination hall and at the healing clinic. I never for one mo-ment thought that it was some wise discarnate entity come to my assistance and yet my impression was the "I" did not write that fourth answer or control my hands as they moved over the patients. I, as observing subject, could see what was done but I, as conscious agent, could not feel responsible for what was taking place.

It is very understandable that this sort of situation can be confusing and difficult to interpret. Perhaps if I had had a different background I might have assumed that I was being "taken over" by some discarnate healer "on the other side" or, alternatively, that I was being moved directly by God or the Holy Spirit. When Hindus speak of hearing the Lord's commands when kundalini reaches the chakra between the eyebrows, they mean the commands of Brahman self speaking for Brahman from within one's own being. It seems to be more difficult for Christians to think of "the still small voice" as coming from part of themselves. It is equally hard sometimes to believe that we are responsible for some of our own best performances. I well understand how the Greeks came to invent the Muses.

While owing many insights to Tantric Hinduism in making sense of my own experience, in this particular area I have found the Christian categories the more helpful if somewhat unconventionally construed. God for me is the universal reality of which the divine potential within each one of us is a singular instance, an individualized fragment. The Holy Spirit is the power by means of which God becomes embodied in the creation; that which, in human beings, enables us to manifest godliness physically in time and space. Christ represents the

end product of the embodying process, the pro-
totype of an individual who is both divine and
human, in whom no vestige of conditioning remains to impede the emergence of the subliminal
self as an incarnation of God in flesh and blood.
This is the Trinity interpreted psychologically.

Buddhism and Vedanta, perhaps because they are
more preoccupied with transcendence than incarnation, do not offer categories so easily adapted to
Western religious psychology as those of Christianity. There seems to be no Hindu equivalent to the
Holy Spirit as a force involved in incarnating the
divine, though the Shakti of yoga operates similarly
to facilitate transcendence as a movement out of the
body. Even Tantric Hinduism, which gives much
importance to the body's role in its yoga and ritual
practices, does not offer us a psychology of incarnation that can be applied to the individual as simply as the Christian one. The orientation towards
transcendence in order to be free from suffering and
rebirth is too native to Indian thought.

What confuses the issue for many people is the
Church's identification of Jesus the man with Christ,
the Second Person of the Trinity, who is also the
divine potential immanent in human beings. It is
because of this identification that theories about the
historical Jesus can be used to diminish the status
and symbolic significance of the Christ. The historical Jesus did not claim for himself the univer-
sality that latter-day Christianity claimed for him.
What he did claim was that he was one with the
Father—in other words, that he had personally
reached the Christ state in which the human and

divine are one. Moreover, he did not claim that only he could do this. He not only exhorted others to follow in his footsteps but said that they could do even greater things because of his achievement. And this is surely true, for each bit of God, each Christ within, that becomes fully incarnated must enrich the whole of mankind and make it easier for others to reach the same goal. It may be easier because of Jesus but it is possible at all because of the Christ potential inherent in us all. Only by distinguishing between Jesus and Christ in this way can we really make sense of the statements that Christ was incarnate in Jesus and that He is also a member of the Trinity present "from the foundation of the world."

The Christ within each individual, seen in this way, is the Christian equivalent of the subliminal self, while the Holy Spirit is the force that enables the subliminal self to overcome the deformities caused by our conditioning and our mistaken judgments. It is what finally ensures that we can all say, "My Father and I are one." This is the consummation of human evolution seen in religious terms.

While making these distinctions—so necessary to clarify my own ideas—I am well aware that the divine within responds to calls upon it without seeming to mind at all what name it is given. So ready is this response once we learn to turn to it that I have known it to answer questions even before they are clearly framed. Of course, we make mistakes while learning to relate to it properly. We may become confused about what comes from it and what from unconscious areas where hopes and fears can gather around themselves subpersonalities often claiming to be famous people or lofty spiritual beings. Those with mediumistic tendencies need to be particularly aware that the "testing of spirits" is no easy matter. The point is that it is better to make mistakes in order to manifest that bit of God entrusted to us than to keep it in perpetual transcendence, worshipping Christ without incarnating Him. And Christianity is nothing if it is not a religion about incarnation. For the best part of two thousand years the Church has tried to fit Christ into a specific institution. Perhaps it is time that we began to think of "the community of all faithful people" not as a body of Christian church-goers but as all people of all religions who try to incarnate God, each in his or her own way, through their personal lives.

And perhaps it would also help to counter the dominance of competitive masculinity in world affairs if we gave more thought to the significance of the Madonna in religious psychology, particularly the Mary of the New Testament. Mary, however revered, has never been given divine status in her own right as an essential participant in the incarnation process. Jung and others have deplored the psychological effects of the identification of the divine with the masculine and welcomed the Assumption of the Virgin as a step in the right direction. I agree about the one-sidedness the Church's stress on the masculine has caused but feel the distortion has historical roots and is not inherent in Christianity itself. A number of factors may have combined to bring it about in the course of the development of the Church as an institution. One, of which we hear singularly little, is the transformation of the Jewish Spirit of God, the Shekinah, into the Holy Spirit as a masculine member of the Christian Trinity. Among the Jews, of whom Jesus was one, this in- dwelling presence has always been thought of as feminine. I do not know at what point nor as the result of what thinking the Christian Spirit of God became masculine. I suspect that it may have been due to a naturalistic approach to the story of Jesus' birth in the first chapter of St. Matthew's gospel. How, some might well have asked, could Jesus be "conceived of the Holy Spirit" if the Holy Ghost were feminine? The entire controversy of the virgin birth seems to be based on a misconception about how the parts of the gospel dealing with the An- nunciation should be interpreted.

There is a little-known doctrine that suggests that the concept of the Shekinah as the Spirit of God may have become split at some stage in the development of Christian thought, its creative and transforming functions becoming incorporated in the Holy Ghost while its femininity was transferred to Mary. Ac- cording to this teaching, while no man can reach God save by Christ, it is also true that no man can reach Christ save by Mary. Psychologically, this is a very illuminating doctrine, for the Mary of the gospels was a completely human person, excep- tional only in being "immaculate," free from all the blemishes that disfigure the humanity of lesser mortals. She is the exemplar of what a human be- ing must be if he or she hopes to bring to birth the potential Christ within. Translating this into the language of Sri Aurobindo, Mary must have achieved the state in which her subliminal self

could work in her from within and she could accept its authority: "Be it unto me according to thy
word." It is this that makes Mary a perfect example of how one must learn to live if one hopes fully
to incarnate the Christ in oneself. I imagine that this
is what is meant by the teaching that one can reach
Christ only through Mary.

I think that a lot of us try to bypass the Mary stage,
and perhaps the way in which the gospels have
been edited and interpreted over the centuries has
been largely responsible for this. Christ and Jesus
have been fused and put "out there," and Mary has
been turned into the Blessed Virgin and a kind of
intercessor-in-chief. The doctrine of the vicarious
atonement is a natural corollary of the projection
outward of Christ as the redeeming principle, and
the identification of the historical Jesus with the
Second Person of the Trinity has placed the redemp-
tive act in a particular moment of time. There are
many who believe that the coming of Jesus represented a turning point in the spiritual life of the
planet. Even if this is so, this fact does not make
good the loss of emphasis on the redeeming power
of the Christ within each and every human being.
It is too easy to put confession and absolution in
place of living the Mary life, to feel that it is sufficient to thank and worship Christ for having made
remorse and penance all that is required of us. To
be forgiven in advance is no incentive to become
sinless, and good works done in the outside world
are not psychologically equivalent to fighting the
good fight against all that is preventing the emergence of the subliminal self. One has only to look
at the decline of the power of the Church in the

modern world to realize that religion has an inner dimension that we are handling very inadequately.

It should also be remembered that many subliminal selves are incarnated in feminine bodies. This is something that Hinduism understands better than either Islam or Christianity. Goddesses abound and are worshipped as such by men and women alike. Only part of the Christian Church offers prayers to the Madonna. The Protestant denominations make little of her except at Christmas. As Jung pointed out, the Western world suffers badly for its emphasis on the masculine at the expense of the feminine, since what is femininely receptive is as vital to life as what is masculinely executive. Wholeness in both humans and societies depends upon a balance of opposites, of complementary forces working together. If they are to be creative, the tension that this involves must never lead to a conflict in which one side wins—as so often happens at present—or, in the long run, both sides lose.

If the subliminal self is the proper form of the personality, it is neither body, mind, nor spirit but a mixture of all three. It shares with the superficial self access to the body and to the individual's memory and skills. For much of our evolution it must operate like the wider half of a split personality. In such cases there is usually one part that knows all that goes on while the other knows only what happens when it is occupying the body itself. The conditioned part of us suffers the same limitations vis a vis the subliminal self. The difference between the enlightened person and the pathological case is that the former is aware of a wider self and the latter is not. Even in unenlightened states we can become aware of it and catch glimpses of the rare possibilities inherent in human nature. And because the body reacts in phase with our inner attitudes and objectives, the more we become conscious of our potentialities, the easier it is for the body to demonstrate them through our outward behavior.

As we have seen, genetic and social factors exert pressures that pull us in various directions in the course of our development into adults. In the process the body remains all of a piece, while we enact a variety of not always consistent roles. It matures according to its own blueprint. Meanwhile, deep within us, we carry another blueprint, more complex than that of the body but containing it. It is our proper form, the blueprint laid down by the subliminal self of the divinely intended person that it must try to manifest in the physical world through us. The ideal situation is one in which the two blueprints have combined to produce an integrated embodied self that is also all of a piece. No hangups, no partial selves playing conflicting roles and setting up civil wars or uneasy coexistences in the same skin—this is the goal of Tantric yoga, also called kundalini yoga. It is only if kundalini forces in the body are capable of actualizing the subliminal self that the yogi can be both enlightened and physically healthy at one and the same time. In Christian terms, it is only the person who can embody the subliminal or Christ self who can say "My Father and I are one" and yet live as a fully human being in the everyday world.

This raises the problem of our muddled and divided selves, the selves with which we are all too familiar. It underlines how important it is to understand our inner conflicts in order that we may live more happily with ourselves and simultaneously enjoy better health. Also it is essential to remember that the body is an inherent part of the self in its proper form. Its instinctive life is normally independent from the conscious part of the self with which we identify. It can only be upset indirectly through the misuse of thought and feeling. It is unhealthy psychic patterns that lead to the weakening of the immune system, to infections, or, alternatively, to psychosomatic disorders.

Of all the bodily systems it is the immune defense system that exemplifies and maintains individual uniqueness at the physical level. The phenomenon of resistance to organ transplants and alien skin grafts is evidence of this. A genetic mechanism may well account for the specificity of fingerprints and even cell structure. It can hardly explain the many psychosomatic interactions in which the immune system participates, which preserve our personal identity from moment to moment. Here there must be an extremely complex interplay of energies within a field polarized between some center of selfhood and the physical body. This is what makes kundalini so important.

As we saw when discussing the relation between kundalini and higher energies in chapter 7, its realm, according to the Tantric texts, is that of physical matter. It is responsible for form and function being so matched that the forces of life and mind can be expressed through chemical structures. It is kundalini that gives solidity to our world.

Without its endless organizing and reorganizing of atoms and molecules our familiar surroundings would volatilize and disappear.

In *Kundalini in the Physical World* I analyzed kundalini, "the threefold Goddess" of Tantric literature, into three groups of forces, which reflect the three major tasks kundalini structures must perform. They must give forms solidity; they must make them capable of exhibiting life; and they must ensure that they can manifest intelligence in adapting to their surroundings. Working together, these three forces maintain physical structures as stable entities each with its own role in a complex but orderly physical universe. They must also contrive that all the needs of a multilevel evolutionary process are met by producing new forms capable of exhibiting even more life and capable of increasingly more complicated feats of adaptation.

The kundalini forces in human beings that maintain our bodies as stable and continuing entities are called homeostatic forces in biology. They operate subconsciously. It is their job to keep our bodies in good working order—keeping temperature and chemical thresholds within normal limits and seeing that the immune system keeps foreign invaders at bay. It is these forces that combine with physical prana in all organic processes. In inanimate forms kundalini works chiefly at molecular and atomic levels to produce the various orders of minerals. The kundalini forces responsible for structures that can handle mental energies I termed "chit-kundalini forces." *Chit* is a Sanskrit word meaning "consciousness" or "intelligence." These forces result in organisms that can respond adaptively to their environment. They give human behavior its plasticity and scope for creativity. It is through the immune system that this combination of forces is individualized to react uniquely in each of us so that no two embodied selves are ever exactly the same.

It is difficult to explain the extreme specificity of immune reactions in terms of Western science or of epiphenomenal theories of personality. Individuality seems as inherent in nature as intelligence or order. It must come from somewhere. I cannot really accept that blind chance put so much uniqueness together so tidily as a result of the random interplay of the products of a Big Bang. In any case what set off the Big Bang and what exploded? The Hindu conception of Brahman as a phenomenally transcendent One fragmenting itself in order to create a play for its own enjoyment (bangs and all) is not only more attractive but, when divested of its poetry, makes better common sense than randomness or an exclusively physical universe.

One of the names given to transcendent Brahman is Satchitananda. *Sat* translates as being or essence, *chit* as intelligence or consciousness, and *ananda* as bliss or joy. The implication is that underlying the creation are all these ingredients. In willing to manifest phenomenally the One reproduces its own fundamental nature insofar as this can be achieved in mind, life, and matter and expressed through physical forms. The uniqueness of created things derives from the fact that each is a separate frag-

ment of manifesting Brahman. The unity of the created universe derives from its origin in the One, the
Many being merely its phenomenal expression in
time and space. Its coherence and order derive from
the same source.

The mystery from this point of view is how disorder and conflict found their way into an intel-
ligently conceived and orderly universe. This
question is continually asked and in the nature of
things can never be answered. One can, however,
suspect that it was necessary at some stage to in-
troduce a tension of opposites in order to convert
a state into a process. This is implied in Genesis
by the arrival of the serpent in the Garden of Eden
in our own creation myth. The allegory of the Fall
implies not only that human beings must be separated from God in order to know Him but also that
they must suffer in order to grow up. Unless one
assumes a creator who cannot handle his creation,
one must believe that the Fall was intended and
necessary for the evolution of consciousness and
self-awareness.

The creative tension in human beings can be seen
as that between the subliminal self as a fragment
of Brahman manifesting itself through a particular
body and the superficial self as the limiting conditions with which it has to contend. It is important
to remember that the body is common to both these
selves and shares in the tension. As part of the subliminal self it seeks health and wholeness. This is
because the subliminal self represents our implicit
wholeness at all levels. It knows its divinely in-

tended role and what the proper form of the personality should be. It works in our lives to correct distortions and heal divisions. It can do this, however, only to the extent that the superficial self will allow. This is because the power and freedom of the superficial self are very real so long as we identify with it and allow it to dominate our actions.

11
Incarnating the True Self

For all its nuisance value as a generator of problems the superficial self is vital to the evolution of consciousness. Its task would seem to be to make us self-aware and ultimately aware of our true nature. It enables us to do this with increasing insight as we struggle with ourselves and with life. It is through it that we learn the hard way the sort of people we really are, our proper values, and our most fitting roles. By its very inadequacies it entices us to modify our atittudes and improve the quality of our lives. It brings us to the point where, as the tension within us lessens, we can catch glimpses of the subliminal self waiting quietly to emerge.

That we take so long to find it is understandable, for the subliminal self is necessarily a bit of a mystery. This is because it is so much larger than our ordinary, workaday selves that it can never be fully known to them. This is particularly maddening for the rationalists among us who want to know all about things before they can believe in them. This is what makes atheists of many of them. Since they cannot accept the idea of a God without, it is hard for them to experience a God within. Mystical insights either elude them or pass unrecognized for what they are. Whether we like it or not, however, consciousness is forever pointing beyond itself, and life is constantly presenting us with mysteries. It is this that makes it possible for the conscious mind to grow and expand. We are impelled from within ourselves to evolve as persons on the one hand and to extend the frontiers of our known world on the other.

Before we can approach the mystery of the subliminal self, however, we must first solve the mystery of our ordinary selves. It is to this that our expanding self-awareness must address itself. In chapter 5 we discussed Arkle's theory of filters, a set of attitudes and ideas by means of which we evaluate experience. It will be recalled that he postulated a first-order filter that most of us are not aware of. This filter, which he called our real being, would be the subliminal self filtering experience in accordance with our karma. It would ensure that we are presented with appropriately testing circumstances and challenges. The second-order filter is the conscious part of the superficial self when it is detached enough to examine its own behavior. We must be able to use this filter if we are ever to solve the mystery of ourselves and ultimately of our relation to the subliminal self. It is only as we develop this capacity for discrimination and self-evaluation that the evolution of consciousness can really take place. Prior to that most of us live in terms of our third-order filter. Our lives are governed by gut feelings and socially acceptable norms. At this stage we do not think very much about anything that stretches the imagination or runs counter to the ideas and values of the groups to which we belong.

When we come to examine ourselves seriously with our second-order filters, we make some unexpected discoveries. Perhaps the most surprising is the realization that, for all its influence on our actions, the self that we think we are is just that. It is an artificial mental construct, a complex of attitudes and ideas that we have about ourselves. It is not an external reality but an inner filter. Psychologists call it a "self-portrait" or "self-image," a creation of the mind based on judgments that we have made about ourselves in the course of growing up. It is usually the result of other people's treatment of us in childhood. It can be fairly true to life or quite false. We may be swans who think that we are ugly ducklings or pompous asses who think we are God's gift to the human race. When we look into our actual experience, we find that the only "I" that is truly real is that sliver of ourselves that is focused in the present. Unlike our self-portraits, which are relatively stable, this "I" is constantly changing as one segment of our personality after another takes the stage. It is not a complex. It is more like a lens that focuses the attention of consciousness on what is there to be attended to. It is the part of us that is, at least in principle, in the Now.

This "I"—often painted as an eye—is important for two reasons. It is the only part of us that is in the present, and it is only in the present that anything can be changed. It is also important because,

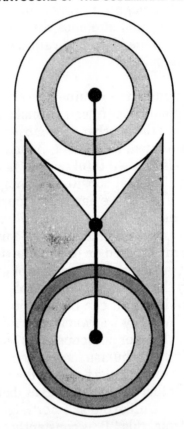

Fig. 5. The Relationships among
Different Aspects of the Self.

The upper circles represent the thinking-intuitive self,
and the lower circles the feeling-instinctive self. The dot
near the middle stands for the mobile center of attention or existential "I." Ideally it is in direct communication both upwards and downwards, in contact with the
subconscious as well as the superconscious. The
triangles on the right and left of it represent negative
areas into which it can be pushed, destroying the alignment of the three aspects of the total self.

in altering our decisions or modifying our behavior, the role of attention is crucial. Both our deformities and their cure are the result of the things to which we give priority, what we attend to. Much more effective than our strenuous efforts to change is to see everything in a new light. As Maurice Nicoll points out in *The Mark*, the Greek word translated as repentance in the Bible is *metanoia*, which literally means "seeing in a new way." That is why repentance is essential to forgiveness and being able "to go and sin no more." It is not penance and punishment that make it possible for us to forgive ourselves and others. It is not gritting our teeth and fighting ourselves that makes us virtuous. It is quite simply seeing our situation in a new light. It is enough to change the focus of attention; and everything is changed.

The trouble is that it is not easy to know exactly what to attend to, and a great deal of time and effort are spent by spiritually minded people in trying to find a way of seeing that will light them on their way. Here again, what Jesus said is simple. What is needed is not blood, sweat, and tears but merely to ask. Perhaps this advice seems naive and altogether too easy to our sophisticated modern minds, especially in the Protestant West. Nevertheless, it is based on psychological truth supported by physiological facts.

When we look at a situation and judge it to be dangerous, we respond to it either as fearful or as challenging, according to our temperaments. This response is not just emotional. Our nerves and glands react differently in the two cases. Put in terms of dense and subtle bodies, the two conscious attitudes generate quite distinct patterns of activity in the chakras. As a result, they feed energy into the glands and nervous system in ways that send quite different messages to the nerve centers in the brain. These in turn send different instructions to the organs and tissues. As a result, we either feel miserable and cringe or feel excited and ready for anything. These two sets of responses are triggered by acts of perception, not by the situation itself. The situation is neutral. It is the conscious self that can interpret it in different ways.

To see life as an adventure is not something that we can do easily if we have been conditioned to distrust ourselves and others. The older we are, the more difficult it becomes, because we have established pathways along which energy habitually flows. The work being done to reeducate disabled people, however, has shown that energy pathways can be changed even in the most adverse circumstances. Disabled people are increasingly being invited to cooperate in their treatment by talking to injured parts and encouraging them to heal themselves. In the present case we are asking the body to heal itself, and we can help it by visualizing the injured parts in good working order. The amount that therapists can do is limited, but it is a great advance that doctors are beginning to see how much more can be done by treating patients as persons who can participate positively in their own treatment. The idea that the real healer is within the patient has still to become explicit in the minds of the medical profession, but fortunately their zeal to improve on their own performance is leading them inexorably in this direction, as the growth of holistic medicine clearly shows.

The relation between the subliminal self and the superficial self with its deformities and inadequacies is very similar to that between the robust healthy part of the patient and his disability. The part that is whole needs to be invoked in order to heal the part that is not. The process must involve, first of all, seeing the situation positively—not seeing ourselves as damaged and becoming hopeless but as capable of regeneration and taking the necessary steps. Taking the necessary steps includes asking, whether we are asking to be able to walk again or asking to grow into wise and integrated people. In both cases, moreover, we must be prepared to accept that whole-making takes time and patience—and, perhaps most of all, persistence and courage. The difference is that asking the subliminal self to make us whole is far easier than asking the body to heal itself. This is because talking to the body, visualizing it as cured, treating it sensibly, and feeding it properly are all jobs that must be directed consciously. Asking the subliminal self for help is a simple matter of recollecting its presence—attending to it—and consciously putting our problems to it. It is not up to us to oversee its responses. Our attention is vital, but our roles are not executive. All we have to do is to be sensitive to its intuitive promptings and let them direct us to sources of help and methods of contact. I did not set out to heal or to paint; I simply found myself in situations where these gifts could emerge.

I am sure that this is the kind of asking to which Jesus referred. And the reason it works is because the whole-maker within, the subliminal self, knows us more intimately than anyone else—far better than the self we identify with, which can be very wrong, as we have seen. If we will let it, the subliminal self will lead us to the outside sources of help best suited to our needs. Our lesser selves tend to seek for the wrong reasons and out of states of mind that veer from ill-informed hope to desperate anxiety. They are impatient and often greedy, wanting to be made whole more rapidly than may be possible. Under their influence we tend to expect others to do more work than we do ourselves, a tendency for which the medical profession is partly to blame but which is nevertheless a form of greed. People seeking spiritual enlightenment are also liable to behave in this way. They join this or that organization, go to this or that popular guru, and expect results more quickly than they can actually be achieved. No outside authority, however exalted, can take the place of the subliminal self as a source of help.

In the spiritual sphere another factor is operative. People may think that they are looking for wholeness or enlightenment when in fact they are after exciting experiences or psychic gifts. This is a very disabling form of greed, because it generates a conflict of interest between the subliminal and superficial selves. It can cause both psychospiritual difficulties and psychosomatic disorders. This is because the dense body and the life vehicle are trying to satisfy two masters. As a result, energy no longer passes smoothly up and down through the chakras. Interference patterns arising in the energy field linking psyche and soma mean that both dense and subtle bodies are put under stress. It is this sort of situation that leads to psychosomatic symptoms or nervous breakdowns if nothing is done about it.

This particular form of tension arising in the course of spiritual development is dealt with in great detail in Alice Bailey's *Esoteric Healing* in sections covering what are called the diseases of mystics and of disciples seeking initiation. C. W. Leadbeater touches briefly on the same subject in *The Chakras*. Alice Bailey's Tibetan teacher goes into it at much greater length and with doctors and psychologists more obviously in mind. When I came to healing, I approached it from both these angles and found his teaching most illuminating and helpful. It enabled me to interpret what my hands were doing from two possible points of view. Some disorders must clearly be understood as cases of bodily malfunctions requiring medical interpretations. Others, however, are best seen as the physical concomitants of energy changes associated with inner growth processes, what Jung would call individuation processes. The latter I found responded better when taken out of a medical context and rethought in terms of spiritual growing pains.

Briefly, the Tibetan teaches that there are polarities between chakral pairs, which change as a person evolves spiritually. The first pair to change in this way are the sacral chakra and the center at the throat. Both these chakras mediate forces concerned with creativity and self-expression, the one through the reproductive organs and the other through speech and communication. At this time one finds energy previously concentrated in a postive sacral center being drawn up into the throat chakra to activate creative energies of a less substantial order. While this polarity change is going on, stresses of various sorts are inevitably generated. Both centers come under strain and behave irregularly. By upward and downward pressures the psyche and the body share in the general reorganization. We can see the consequences in patterns of illness and changes in social behavior. Not only psychological sex problems arise but trouble in the sex organs themselves. Menstrual and menopausal difficulties, infertility and tumors can arise from aberrations at the sacral pole. Disorders of the thyroid and parathyroid glands and pulmonary upsets can indicate imbalances at the opposite pole. The diagnostic problem is to decide whether the origins of illness are to be regarded primarily as physical or primarily as spiritual.

The solar plexus and the heart centers are another linked pair of chakras that have to switch polarities. Gut feelings and self-interest, which dominate behavior at earlier stages of development, are emotions associated with the dominance of the solar-plexus center. Before feelings of compassion and the ideals of social justice can be expressed, dominance must pass from the solar plexus to the heart chakra. The disorders that accompany this protracted and difficult changeover are diseases of the heart and blood vessels on the one hand and a whole range of digestive troubles on the other. From this point of view the widespread incidence of all these disorders could reflect polarity changes occurring on a global scale as an evolutionary phenomenon. The accelerating pace of change that is responsible for so much adaptive stress in these centers may be another evolutionary force. It is compelling our minds and bodies to adjust faster to a wider range of stimuli than ever before in human history. Not all the world's ills should be regarded as pathological. Growing pains are not necessarily confined to individuals.

The incarnation of the subliminal self requires a reversal of polarity between the center at the base of the spine and the one at the top of the head. Before that, however, there must be more activity in the head chakras. A switch is needed from dominance by the centers in the body to dominance by those in the head. In this process the chakra between the eyebrows is said to play an important synthetic role. We must learn to use will and mind to achieve a state of detachment that will make possible the sort of self-awareness I mentioned earlier. We must be able to see ourselves and other people more realistically and not as we want them to be. Until we can attain a state of nonidentification with all that is artificial in our makeup, our true selves cannot emerge. This means emptying ourselves of those parts that hark back to the past and those parts that we have invested in hopes for the future. We must become that "I" that alone is in the present and able to adjust to what is actually there to be dealt with. At all times we must be able to bring to bear just that segment of our total selves needed by the subliminal self for the task in hand. This is no easy undertaking, and we can only achieve it with the help of that same subliminal self whose agent we seek to become.

Sadly, it is far more difficult to convince members of our secular society to turn for help to their subliminal selves than it seems to be for those who come from more religious backgrounds. The hardest thing is to get materialistically minded men and women to believe in its existence, let alone seek its help with the problems of daily living. Even the more spiritually prone can find it difficult if for rather different reasons. Here rationalism is less in evidence than a reluctance of the self with which we have for so long identified to cede any of its sovereignty, largely out of fear of its own unconscious depths. Almost any human guru, psychotherapist, or medium tends to seem a safer alternative. Self-doubt can be another impeding factor.

A long period of patient work is often needed before people can overcome their doubts and misgivings, just as it takes a great deal of patient asking before the disabled person discovers how marvelously the body can respond if asked often enough in the right way. Nevertheless, so long as we keep expecting other people to resolve our difficulties for us, we are never going to ask properly. Healing and regeneration can only be complete if they are our own work, however many of our fellow human beings help us on our way. This is because the whole-maker in each one of us is our own true self seeking incarnation, and it can only succeed in this through us. If we fail it, in a very real sense we fail ourselves.

Not only do I think that our new renaissance depends on our seeing ourselves in the context of this larger person who is our true self, but that to do so has many advantages both for ourselves and for society in general. For the conscious self the biggest bonus is the relaxation that comes from feeling less responsible—less responsible for every act; less responsible for the state of the world. It can stop thinking "Whatever shall I do?" or "It all depends on *me*" or "This isn't going according to plan" or "I *must* make him see it my way." Instead, it can sink back into the subliminal self and say, "What shall *we* do?" and wait for it to precipitate its answer into consciousness.

How it does this varies. Sometimes one just seems to know what to do, whereas before one was full of doubts. Sometimes there is a quiet voice or a clear intuition. Sometimes—and this happens especially when one is a strong personality used to making one's own decisions—one tries a number of "sensible" alternatives that all fail for some reason until only one course is left open. Sometimes the subliminal self teaches us inwardly, but it also seems to use circumstances, not always comfortably, by this method of closing and opening doors. This is a good reason for not trying to force our own or other people's lives into patterns that may seem desirable to us but that may well run counter to the individual destiny each needs to fulfill.

The true self can know what is best not only for us but also for others, because the reality to which it belongs seems to be an unbroken whole in which the wholeness of each of us inheres as an integral part. It knows past, present, and future because in that reality all three seem to be enfolded together in an eternal Now.

Coming to realize that we are part of something that has access to so much wisdom and power over life and time can bring our small ego selves so much release and relief. Our tangled lives, our chaotic world, may not after all be so tangled and chaotic as they seem. God in us and in the world may indeed be working out some purpose that has more order in it than we can presently see. One thing is certain, however, and that is that the more we can believe in and incarnate that fragment of God with which we are entrusted, the sooner an age of peace and goodwill can come into being through us.

And this is true above all for those of us who are given the trusteeship to govern people and nations and to rear and educate the young. I cannot imagine a whole-maker who is either racist or sexist or nationalistically or religiously intolerant. Perhaps the current excesses of terrorists and fanatics serve a more constructive purpose than we realize, as does the greed that may yet bring the international economic system down in ruins. If, like the pilots in the Battle of Britain, we can learn to say, when beset on all sides, "Over to you, God. Over," the tide must surely turn. For to know that, as mere mortals, we cannot manage our sorry world alone is both the end of hubris and the beginning of wisdom. If we can see this, the new renaissance should not be long delayed. All that is keeping it back is a perverse myopia that makes us reluctant to see the rich and multidimensional universe in which we live as "the many-splendored thing" it really is. This is the metanoia we need. To rethink ourselves in such a way that we can cooperate as junior partners in a vast concern, partners whose role is vital but whose knowledge and skill are limited. Our job is to grow in wisdom and ability under the direction of our subliminal selves until such time as we can share the vision of the senior partners we as yet encounter all too seldom. The task is not easy, but the rewards are incalculable.

Bibliography

Arkle, W. 1974. *A Geography of Consciousness*. London: Neville Spearman.

Aurobindo, Sri. 1976. *The Synthesis of Yoga*. 6th ed. Pondicherry, India: Sri Aurobindo Ashram Trust.

Bailey, Alice A. 1925. *A Treatise on Cosmic Fire*. London, New York: Lucis Press.

————. 1942. *Esoteric Psychology*. London, New York: Lucis Press.

————. 1953. *Esoteric Healing*. London, New York: Lucis Press.

Bendit, P. D. and L. J. Bendit. 1943. *The Psychic Sense*. London: Faber and Faber.

————. 1957. *Man Incarnate*. Wheaton, IL: Theosophical Publishing House.

Bentov, I. 1977. *Stalking the Wild Pendulum*. New York: E. P. Dutton & Company.

Bernstein, M. 1956. *The Search for Bridey Murphy*. New York: Doubleday.

Bird, C. 1978. *Divination*. London: Macdonald & Janes.

Blavatsky, H. P. 1978 (1893). *The Secret Doctrine*. Adyar, Madras, India: Theosophical Publishing House.

Bleibtreu, J. M. 1968. *The Parable of the Beast*. London: Gollancz.

Bohm, D. 1980. *Wholeness and the Implicate Order*. London: Routledge and Kegan Paul.

Burr, H. S. 1972. *Blueprint for Immortality*. London: Neville Spearman.

Cade, C. M. and N. Coxhead. 1979. *The Awakened Mind*. Godalming, England: Wildwood House.

163

Castaneda, C. 1968. *The Teachings of Don Juan*. London: Penguin; Berkeley, CA: University of California Press.

————. 1971. *A Separate Reality*. London: Penguin; Berkeley, CA: University of California Press.

————. 1973. *Journey to Ixtlan*. London: Penguin; Berkeley, CA: University of California Press.

Cayce, H. L. 1964. *Venture Inward*. London, New York: Harper & Row.

Cerminara, G. 1950. *Many Mansions*. New York: William Sloane Associates.

Cousens, G. 1986. *Spiritual Nutrition*. Boulder, CO: Cassandra Press.

Crookall, R. 1960. *The Study and Practice of Astral Projection*. London: Aquarian Press.

————. 1964. *The Techniques of Astral Projection*. London: Aquarian Press.

Cruden, W. V. March 1957. "A study of wake." London: *The Lancet*.

Droscher, V. B. 1967. *The Magic of the Senses*. London: W. H. Allen; New York: Dutton.

Dunlap, Jane. 1961. *Exploring Inner Space*. New York: Harcourt, Brace and World.

Evans, J. 1986. *Mind, Body and Electromagnetism*. Shaftesbury, England: Element Books.

Ferguson, Marilyn, 1981. *The Aquarian Conspiracy*. London: Routledge and Kegan Paul; Los Angeles: Jeremy P. Tarcher, Inc.

Gardner, A. 1935. *Vital Magnetic Healing*. London: Transaction of the Theosophical Research Centre.

Garrett, Eileen. 1948. *Adventures in the Supernormal*. New York: Creative Age Press.

Gray's Anatomy. 1980. London: Longmans.

Green, Celia. 1968. *Lucid Dreaming*. London: Hamish Hamilton.

Green, C. and C. McCreery. 1975. *Apparitions*. London: Hamish Hamilton.

Grey, Margot. 1985. *Return from Death*. London: Routledge and Kegan Paul.

Gurney, E., F. Myers, and F. Podmore. 1886. *Phantasms of the Living.* London: Trubner.

Hardy, Sir A. 1975. *The Biology of God.* London: Collins.

Hasted, J. 1981. *The Metal Benders.* London: Routledge and Kegan Paul.

Humphreys, G. W. and M. J. Riddoch. 1987. To See But Not to See: A Case Study of Visual Agnosia. Hove, England: Lawrence Erlbaum Associates.

Huxley, A. 1954. *The Doors of Perception.* London: Chatto and Windus.

Jung, C. G. 1940. *The Integration of Personality.* London: Kegan Paul, Trench and Trubman; also in *Development of Personality. Collected Works,* Bollingen Series XX, Volume 17, 1981. Princeton, NJ: Princeton University Press.

―――. 1958. *Psychology and Religion: West and East.* London: Routledge and Kegan Paul; New Haven, CT: Yale University Press, 1938.

―――. 1960. *Structure and Dynamics of the Psyche.* London: Routledge and Kegan Paul; *Collected Works,* Bollingen Series XX, Volume 8, 1981. Princeton, NJ: Princeton University Press.

―――. 1963. *Memories, Dreams, Reflections.* A. Jaffe, ed. London: Collins and Routledge and Kegan Paul; New York: Random House, 1965.

Karagulla, S. 1967. *Breakthrough to Creativity.* Santa Monica, CA: De Vorss.

Kilner, W. 1911. *The Human Atmosphere or Aura Made Visible by Chemical Means.* Re-issued under the title *The Human Aura;* New York: University Books, 1965.

Krippner, S. and D. Rubin. 1973. *Galaxies of Life.* New York: Gordon and Breach.

Kübler-Ross, E. 1970. *On Death and Dying.* London: Tavistock Publications; New York: Macmillan, 1969.

Leadbeater, C. W. 1987 (1902). *Man, Visible and Invisible.* Wheaton, IL: Theosophical Publishing House.

―――. 1987 (1927). *The Chakras.* Abridged. Wheaton,

IL: Theosophical Publishing House.

————. 1919. *Occult Chemistry*. London: Theosophical Publishing House.

Long, M. F. 1948. *The Secret Science behind Miracles*. Los Angeles: Kosmon Press.

Lorimer, David. 1984. *Survival: Body, Mind and Death in the Light of Psychic Experience*. London: Routledge and Kegan Paul.

Millard, J. 1956. *Edgar Cayce, Mystery Man of Miracles*. New York: Fawcett Publications.

Monroe, R. A. 1972. *Journeys out of the Body*. London: Souvenir Press; New York: Doubleday.

Moody, R. A. 1975. *Life after Life*. New York: Mockingbird Press, Bantam Books.

Motoyama, H. 1981. *Theories of the Chakras*. Wheaton, IL: Theosophical Publishing House.

Muldoon, S. and H. Carrington. 1956. *Projections of the Astral Body*. London: Rider.

Nicoll, M. 1954. *The Mark*. London: Vincent Stuart.

Northrop, F. S. C. and H. S. Burr. 1935. "An electrodynamic theory of life." *Quarterly Review of Biology*. Vol. 10, pp. 322-33.

Osborn, A. W. 1961. *The Future is Now: The Significance of Precognition*. Wheaton, IL: Theosophical Publishing House.

Ostrander, S. and L. Schroeder. 1973. *Psi: Psychic Discoveries behind the Iron Curtain*. London: Abacus; Englewood Cliffs, NJ: Prentice-Hall, Inc., 1970.

Pearce, I. 1983. *The Gate of Healing*. Saffron Waldon, England: C. W. Daniel.

Pelletier, K. R. 1978. *Mind as Healer, Mind as Slayer*. London: George Allen and Unwin.; Magnolia, MA: Smith, Peter Pub., Inc., 1984.

Penfield, Wilder. 1975. *The Mysteries of Mind*. Princeton, NJ: Princeton University Press.

Phillips, S. 1986. "ESP of atoms." *Theosophical Research Journal*, Vol. 3, No. 4.

Powell, A. E. 1928. *The Etheric Double*. London: Theosophical Publishing House.

Pribram, K. 1971. *Languages of the Brain*. Englewood Cliffs, NJ: Prentice-Hall.

Progoff, I. 1964. *The Image of an Oracle: Research into the Mediumship of Eileen Garrett*. New York: Helix Press.

Puharich, A. 1962. *Beyond Telepathy*. London: Darton, Long and Todd; New York: Anchor Press, 1973.

Ravitz, L. J. 1959. "Application of electro-dynamic field theory in biology, psychiatry and hypnosis." *Amer. J. of Clinical Hypnosis*, Vol. 1, No. 4, April.

Rhine, J. B. and J. G. Pratt. 1957. *Parapsychology: Frontier Science of Mind*. Springfield, IL: Thomas.

Robinson, E. 1977. *The Original Vision*. Oxford: Religious Experience Research Unit.

————. 1978. *Living the Questions*. Oxford: Religious Experience Research Unit.

Russell, E. 1971. *Design for Destiny*. London: Neville Spearman.

Ryall, E. W. 1974. *Second Time Round*. London: Neville Spearman.

Ryzl, M. 1962. "Training the psi faculty by hypnosis." *J. Soc. Psychical Research*, Vol. 41, No. 11, pp. 234-52.

————. 1966. "A method of training in ESP." *Int. J. Parapsychology*, Vol. 8, No. 4.

Sacks, O. 1985. *The Man who Mistook his Wife for a Hat*. London: Picador/Pan Books; New York: Harper & Row, 1987.

Sannella, L. 1976. *Kundalini: Psychosis or Transcendence*. San Francisco; Dakin.

Scheibel, M. E. and A. B. Scheibel. 1968. "Hallucinations and the brain stem reticular core." *Hallucinations*. London: Grune and Stratton, Inc.

Scott, Mary. 1983. *Kundalini in the Physical World*. London: Routledge and Kegan Paul.

Sinclair, Upton. 1930. *Mental Radio*. Pasadena, CA: Pasadena Station.

Smith, Justa. 1973. ''Paranormal effects of enzyme activity.'' *Human Dimensions*. Vol. 2, No. 1.

Soal, S. G. and F. Bateman. 1954. *Modern Experiments in Telepathy*. London: Faber.

Steiner, Rudolf. 1932. *Occult Physiology*. London: Rudolf Steiner Press; New York: Anthroposophic Press.

————. 1962. *Occult Science* (new translation). London: Rudolf Steiner Press; New York: Anthroposophic Press, Inc., 1969.

Stevenson, I. 1966. *Twenty Cases Suggestive of Reincarnation*. Charlottesville, VA: University Press of Virginia.

Teilhard de Chardin, P. 1959. *The Phenomenon of Man*. London: Collins; New York: Harper.

Thigpen, C. H. and H. M. Cleckdey. 1957. *The Three Faces of Eve*. New York: McGraw Hill.

Thomas, Lewis. 1974. *The Lives of a Cell*. New York: Viking Press.

Underwood, G. 1972. *The Pattern of the Past*. London: Abacus.

van der Post, L. 1958. *The Lost World of the Kalahari*. London: Hogarth Press/Penguin; San Diego: Harcourt Brace Jovanovich, 1977.

————. 1961. *The Heart of the Hunter*. London: Hogarth Press/Penguin; San Diego: Harcourt Brace Jovanich, 1980.

Vasiliev, L. L. 1963. *Experiments in Distant Influence*. Godalming, Surrey: Wildwood House.

————. 1963. *Experiments in Mental Suggestion*. London: Gally Hill Press.

Walter, W. G. 1953. *The Living Brain*. London: Duckworth.

White, E., ed. 1972. *The Highest State of Consciousness*. New York: Anchor Books, Doubleday.

White, R. and M. Swainson. 1979. *The Healing Spectrum*. London: Neville Spearman.

Whiteman, J. H. M. 1961. *The Mystical Life*. London: Faber and Faber.

Wilber, K., ed. 1982. *The Holographic Paradigm*. Boston: Shambhala.

Wolstenholme, G. E. W. and J. Knight, eds. 1971. *The Pineal Gland: A Ciba Symposium*. Edinburgh, London: Churchill Livingston.

Woodroffe, Sir J. (Arthur Avalon) 1919. *The Serpent Power*. Madras, India: Ganesh.

————. 1920. *Shakti and Shakta*. Madras, India: Ganesh.

Index

About the Author

Mary Scott was born in India where her father was the Principal of Bahaddin College in Kathiawar. Both her parents were theosophists, so that she became interested in esoteric subjects and comparative philosophy while still a teenager. She inherited her father's enquiring mind and, after a short career in nursing, read psychology and philosophy at Edinburgh University, where she gained a gold medal and the Vans Dunlop scholarship in philosophy. With the latter she read for a post-graduate diploma in Social Studies and became a university teacher, first in England and then in Ghana. In Africa she pioneered the first course enabling administrative officers to take their promotion examinations in their own country.

The after-effects of the accident about which she writes in the book led to her giving up full-time teaching to work as a part-time psychologist, lecturer and writer. She is the author of *Kundalini in the Physical World*, which is based on sources in Tantric literature that treat kundalini as a universal force in nature.

Quest publishes books on Healing, Health and Diet, Occultism and Mysticism, Philosophy, Transpersonal Psychology, Reincarnation, Religion, The Theosophical Philosophy, Yoga and Meditation. **Other Quest books include:**

The Astral Body by A. E. Powell
An in-depth study of our subtle bodies.
The Atman Project by Ken Wilber
A transpersonal view of human development.
Between Two Worlds by Frederic Wiedemann
Using the soul to integrate personality with spiritual nature.
Beyond the Post-Modern Mind by Huston Smith
A look beyond reductionism and our materialistic culture.
The Chakras by Charles W. Leadbeater
Illustrated examination of energy centers in the body.
Encounter with Awareness by R. Puligandla
Study of pure consciousness that comprises our essential being.
The Etheric Double by A. E. Powell
The health aura. What it is and what it does.
Evolution of Integral Consciousness by H. Chaudhuri
Study of consciousness as a holistic phenomenon.
Expansion of Awareness by A. W. Osborn
One man's search for meaning in life.
Rhythm of Wholeness by Dane Rudhyar
A study of the continuous process of being.

Available from:
The Theosophical Publishing House
306 West Geneva Road, Wheaton, Illinois 60187